Penguin Garden Centre Guides

Water Gardening

Philip Swindells

PENGUIN BOOKS

Penguin Books Ltd, Harmondsworth, Middlesex, England
Viking Penguin Inc., 40 West 23rd Street, New York, New York 10010, U.S.A.
Penguin Books Australia Ltd, Ringwood, Victoria, Australia
Penguin Books Canada Ltd, 2801 John Street, Markham, Ontario, Canada L3R 1B4
Penguin Books (N.Z.) Ltd, 182–190 Wairau Road, Auckland 10, New Zealand

First published 1985

Edited and designed by Robert Ditchfield Ltd
Illustrated by Emma Tovey

Acknowledgements
The publishers would like to thank the following contributors and copyright owners of the colour photographs:
Gillian and Kenneth Beckett (28 middle, 37 above); Harold Langford (20,
21, 24, 28 top, 36, 40, 41); Lotus Water Garden Products Ltd, 260–300
Berkhamstead Road, Chesham, Bucks, HP5 3EY (17); Diana Saville (4, 5, 9,
13, 25, 28 bottom, 29, 32, 37 below, 44, 45, 53); Stapeley Water Gardens Ltd,
London Road, Stapeley, Nantwich, Cheshire CW5 7LH (48 above and below).

Printed and bound in Italy by New Interlitho, Milan

Typesetting by Keyspools Ltd
Colour separation by RCS Graphics Ltd

Contents

1. Water in the Garden

Few features can be as attractive in the garden as water. In its various moods it conveys many things. A still pool reflecting all about it has a serene calmness. The whispering of water over rock creates a romantic mood, while the crashing fury of a millrace reminds us of the vigour and impetuousness of youth. Thus it appeals to everyone in some way, for not only is water a fascinating medium, but one in which a whole new array of plants can be grown. Not only that, but the watery canvas which the garden artist creates can be enlivened with fish which give an added dimension scarcely apparent in the rest of the garden. Butterflies and birds help make the garden scene but they are transitory and fickle; whereas the fish are confined but not unpleasantly so, and with their antics provide continuing amusement for both young and old. Many is the gardener who has been bitten by the fish-keeping bug and become a devotee of aquaria, but that is another story.

Siting the pool

It is very important from the start to select a suitable position for the pool, for once installed it is difficult to move. It is not possible to create the pool in as off-hand a manner as a rose bed, for the latter can be moved in the autumn and one would scarcely know. A pool is more permanent and so is its ecology. Disturb the watery environment and it will take a couple of years to regain its harmony. Visually it is important where the pool is placed, but horticulturally it is even more vital. For healthy plant growth to result, it is essential to have the pool in an open sunny position. All aquatics enjoy full sun and will prosper in such a situation, creating the ideal conditions for a healthy natural balance. Fish also like sunshine, providing that there are a few waterlily pads under which to glide during the heat of a summer day. Shelter is useful, for taller marginal plants are not very stable even when growing in a proper container; a stiff

An oriental summerhouse is the focal point in this large but simply planted water garden.

breeze will often topple them into the deep area with unpleasant consequences. The ideal place for a garden pool is therefore in full sun and sheltered from the prevailing wind.

An ideal position is not always easy to find, but any situation near trees should be avoided. Not only do trees provide undesirable shade, but also falling leaves decompose in the water and release noxious gases. Netting the pool during autumn, just prior to leaf fall, is a useful precaution in any event as leaves will often blow into the pool from neighbouring gardens, but the deliberate siting of a pool close by trees is folly. Even weeping trees that are usually associated with water should be avoided, especially the weeping willow. Widely planted beside pools, it is totally unsuited, having foliage that contains a substance akin to aspirin which is extremely toxic to fish. Its roots are invasive too and can cause considerable damage to a concrete pool. The weeping willow is lovely in the right place, and that is beside a river where its roots can spread unimpeded and its toxic foliage is washed away by fast flowing water. Some gardeners have a great desire for a weeping tree beside their pool and select one of the very fine pendulous flowering cherries. However, these are equally unsuited as they are the winter host of the waterlily aphid, a tiresome little pest that attacks succulent aquatic plants in the same way that the black bean aphid devastates broad beans. When planted beside the pool there is no means of spraying the over-wintering generation without polluting the pool. Summer generations are impossible to control chemically without killing the fish. Any flowering cherry should be planted away from the pool so that a liberal tar oil winter wash can be applied.

Having considered the practical aspects of siting the pool, one must consider the visual. Taking nature as an example, water is only found naturally at the lowest point in the landscape and it only looks comfortable in a garden when placed lower than the surrounding area. It is often the case, however, that the lowest part of the garden is unsuitable on practical grounds, in which case a higher area must be dug for it and then the soil from this excavation has to be redistributed to give the appearance that the pool is in fact lower. Only in a formal situation can a pool be raised above the surrounding area and look attractive; the kind of pool, for example, that is made from a raised wall on which one can sit on warm summer days and dabble the fingers. Even if the pool cannot be placed in the perfect position, by careful construction and skilful planting it can be made to work well and provide endless hours of pleasure for its owner.

Even a small pool provides the opportunity to raise fish and grow a variety of plants.

2. Choosing a Design

The design one selects for a pool is a matter for personal choice, but, to conform with the simple rules of landscaping, a formal design should be included in a formal garden while an informal pool must rest in a cottage garden or one of similar appearance.

The natural pool

Few gardeners are blessed with natural water, but those that are should carefully consider their handling of this marvellous asset. Structural and design changes should be minimal as water will have found its level in a natural way and generally little can be done to improve the overall effect. Skilful planting is more likely to improve this asset than major structural alterations. Indeed, the latter can often lead to problems with seepage and may destroy the beauty of the feature.

The formal pool

In a formal garden the surface design of the pool should be square, rectangular, oval or circular, or a combination of these mathematical shapes. Fountains and ornaments should be carefully placed so that the overall effect is one of equilibrium. The materials from which the pool is constructed are also important, for they must be consistent throughout and the lines created, whether by a coping or paving, pronounced and severe. A formal pool can be raised, sunken or built adjacent to a wall without offending nature, for this plays no part in the design of a formal pool. It is when it comes to planting that nature must be persuaded to harmonise. Open water with its reflective qualities is one of the main benefits of water in a formal garden. The long finger-like branches of trees reflected in the water, gentle ripples causing magical distortions, and glowing colours from an autumn sunset are all part of the beauty of a formal pool. The plants are merely used to frame the picture. Not a heavy gilt frame, but a light delicate surround provided by plants with architectural qualities. Open water can sometimes be punctuated with the broad spreading pads of waterlilies, but careful placement is essential if harmony is to be retained.

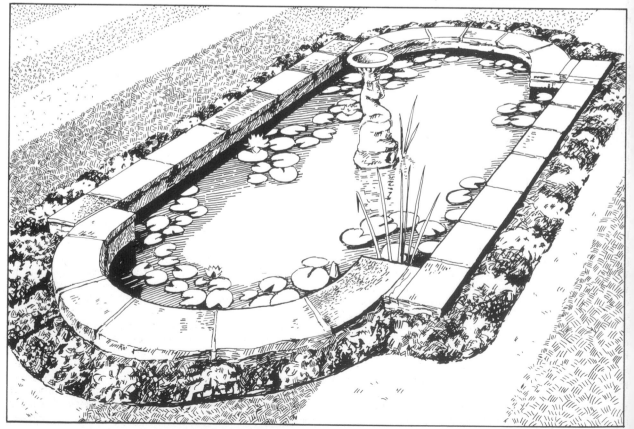

The informal pool

Planting is equally important in an informal pool, for although there may be an appearance of informality this does not just happen. Informal plantings have to be as cleverly contrived as those in a formal pool, for what is essentially an artificial arrangement has to look completely natural. The surface design of an informal pool has no strict rules to follow, for the intention is to recreate something that looks natural, and this can take any fanciful shape the gardener desires. However, it is wise to make a shape of sweeping arcs and radii that can be easily translated in practice into a pool. Fussy niches and contortions should not be permitted as they not only present construction problems, but difficulties with maintenance as well.

The pool surroundings should also conform with the pool and where possible the edge of the pool should be disguised with plants like creeping jenny, rupturewort or brooklime. When a rock garden forms an integral part of the feature, this can be brought right to the edge of the water and, where space permits, may invade a little.

Internal design

It is all very well having a pool that looks good from above, but if the internal structure is not satisfactory it is unlikely to become a feature of great beauty. Various aquatic subjects require different levels at which to grow, the submerged oxygenating plants occupying deep water along with waterlilies and other deep water subjects. Marginal plants naturally inhabit the shallows around the pool, while the different kinds of ornamental fish have varying needs if they are to survive the winter. Shallow pools cannot successfully accommodate any but the common goldfish, and even these need a minimum depth of $1\frac{1}{2}$ ft (45 cm) of water at least at one point in the pool if they are to survive the winter. Similarly, waterlilies and deep water aquatics of the more popular kinds are happier in water of at least $1\frac{1}{2}$ ft (45 cm), but seldom relish more than 3 ft (90 cm). Deeper water greatly restricts the choice of plants that can be used, those that will tolerate these conditions generally having too great a spread for the average garden pool. Marginal plants can grow in a varying depth of water, but most of the popular kinds will prefer no more than 3 ins (8 cm) of water over their crowns. If an allowance is made for the depth of the planting container, a shelf 9 ins (23 cm) deep and the same width must be considered as a minimum requirement. If a concrete or lined pool is to be constructed, it is sensible to contemplate a planting programme and then create conditions for the plants desired, rather than having to select plants afterwards.

3. Pool Liners

Pool liners are one of the easiest and most popular methods of pool construction. Their great advantage is flexibility, allowing the gardener to construct a pool of any fanciful shape that he may desire. Consisting of a sheet of waterproof material which is used to line the excavation, they can be obtained in such a diversity of quality and range of price that there is likely to be one within the reach of the most impecunious gardener.

Polythene liners

The cheapest liners are made of 500 gauge polythene, often in a bright sky blue colour, and in several standard sizes. These are packed in brightly coloured boxes and can be purchased from most sizeable department stores. While being inexpensive, they are the least durable of all, having a life expectancy of little more than three years at the outside. Their great drawback is that they perish unless kept totally immersed in water. This in theory is not a problem, but in practice can cause difficulties, for evaporation from the pool surface regularly lowers the water level and leaves a gap between water level and the surrounding ground. This area of the polythene is very susceptible to perishing and general deterioration, and within a couple of years will break up and effectively leave the lower half of the liner detached from the upper part. The most useful purpose to which this liner can be put is as a small hospital pool for fish or a temporary sanctuary for plants when the pool has to be cleaned out.

PVC liners

Pool liners within the medium price range are usually made of PVC, many incorporating a terylene web as reinforcement. They are available in fairly neutral stone and grey colours, as well as bright blue and ornamental pebble-dash. These have a much longer life than polythene ones, seldom showing signs of deterioration in the first ten or twelve years, although being vulnerable to mechanical damage and puncturing easily if carelessly managed. While also available in standard sizes, these can often be purchased in a specific size that is cut to suit your requirements for a few extra pence.

Rubber liners

Rubber liners are the most permanent of all, and while not indestructible, show no visible signs of deterioration from sunlight or water after a period of time. Of course they are much more expensive than the other two kinds, but this undoubted durability makes them a better investment when a permanent water garden feature is being constructed.

Rubber pool liners are usually black with a matt finish which provides suitable conditions for some of the clinging algae like mermaid's hair to become established. Algae are generally undesirable in the pool, but when restricted to coating the sides of a pool they are very useful. In the case of the rubber liner they hide it almost completely from view, giving the illusion that the pool is completely natural. For those who must have a vivid blue or green pool, special paints are available for use on rubber liners.

Calculating the size

It may seem fairly obvious that the size of the liner will be substantially larger than the excavation, but it is surprising how much larger it turns out to be. It must be remembered that it is not just the overall depth, length and breadth that have to be considered, but also the overlap of up to a foot at the top of the pool for securing it to the ground. If the pool is of an irregular shape, then calculations must be based upon the dimensions of a rectangle which will enclose the most distant edges of the excavation.

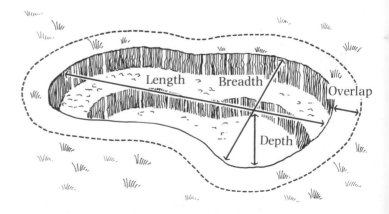

The following formula will give you the size of liner you require:

(twice the depth + length + 2 overlaps) × (twice the depth + breadth + 2 overlaps).

Installing the liner

All liners are installed in a similar manner, except that it must be remembered that polythene liners have little elasticity and should be spread out on the lawn in full sun for a couple of hours before being installed. This makes them much more malleable and amenable to fitting the contours of the excavation.

1. Dig your pool to the shape and depth you require (see pages 6–7). The excavation should then be scoured for any sticks, stones, flints or other sharp objects that may puncture the liner. When these present a serious problem, it is sensible to spread a layer of sand over the pool floor and the marginal shelves and protect the sides of the pool with thick wads of dampened newspaper.

2. As polythene liners have little flexibility they should be placed into the excavation without water being added, allowing plenty of room for movement so that, as it fills, the liner moulds to the exact contours of the excavation. Rubber and PVC liners can be stretched across the excavation and held down with paving slabs or bricks at strategic points.

3. Water is run in and as the liner tightens the anchoring weights are slowly removed until the pool becomes full and the liner moulds to the contours. Wrinkles in the liner should be dealt with as much as possible while the pool is filling.

4. Once full, the surplus material around the edge can be trimmed before being finally secured by paving slabs. As pool liners are not toxic to fish and plant life, they can be stocked almost immediately.

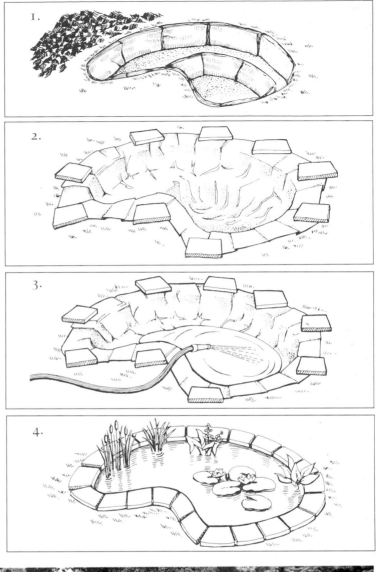

A rubber liner has been used here to make a large pool with an island.

4. The Pre-formed Pool

Pre-formed pools in fibreglass and vacuum-formed plastic are another popular method of creating a water garden. They are permanent, durable and compared with traditional concrete are easy to install. Unfortunately most pre-formed pools are the creations of pool manufacturers and not gardeners, so in many cases accommodation for marginal subjects like rushes and irises is totally inadequate. Study carefully an intended purchase and see that there is a width of at least 9 ins (23 cm) on the marginal shelves and that the bottom of the deeper part of the pool is flat so that flat-bottomed planting baskets can sit on it without tipping.

Plastic or fibreglass?

At the cheaper end of the market there are many pools of plastic construction which are excellent value, light to handle and very durable. However, they are also flexible and this can create difficulties during installation compared with the more expensive fibreglass kinds, which are rigid and free-standing. If finance is available, then the fibreglass kind is unquestionably the better. Apart from shape and structure, colour must be considered, for fibreglass has a smooth surface and does not develop algae freely. Stone or pale green colours would be my choice, but brilliant blue and white are available for those who like them.

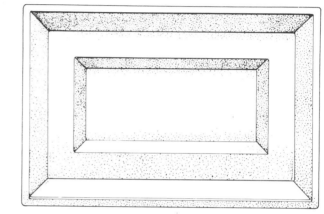

Formal fibreglass pool

Rock pools

Amongst the pre-formed pools are two groups referred to loosely as rock pools and fountain trays. The former are small pools which are often installed as header pools at the summit of a rock garden when it is intended to circulate the water and create a waterfall. Their initial attraction to the unwary is that they are small and cheap, but being shallow they are unsuited to the cultivation of anything except a tiny marginal plant and cannot accommodate aquatic livestock of any kind, except perhaps the odd snail or two. Fountain trays are similarly constructed and totally unsuitable for fish or plant life. These are used for small fountains, more often than not providing a receptacle into which a wall figure or gargoyle can spout.

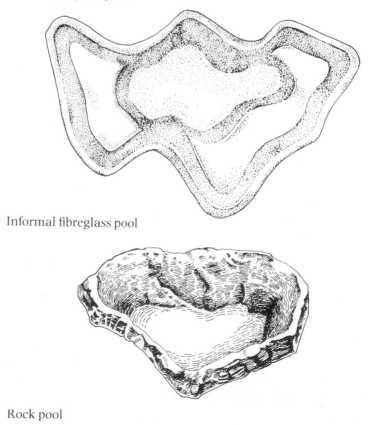

Informal fibreglass pool

Rock pool

Installing the pool

When you buy a fibreglass pool you may assume that you merely dig a hole to the correct shape. This seems logical until you get the pool home and discover how difficult this would be. Such attempts are time-consuming and almost certainly fail. The most practical way of installing a fibreglass pools is as follows:

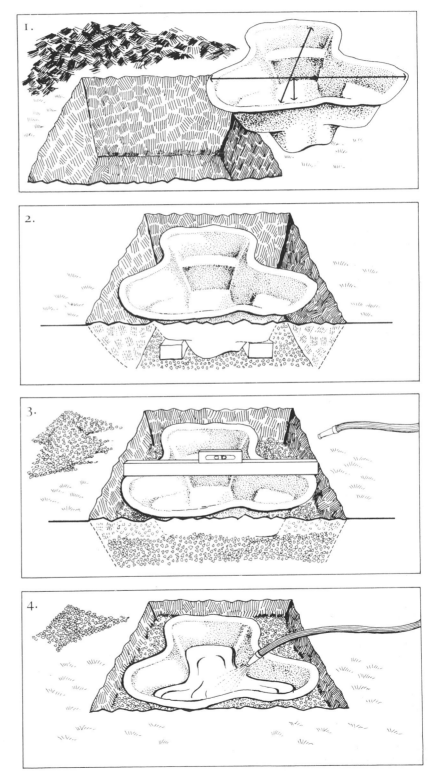

1. Measure the external dimensions and dig a large rectangular hole that more than encloses the pre-formed shape. It is most important that the excavation is sufficiently large to allow for comfortable backfilling once the pool is in place.

2. Cover the floor of the excavation with a layer of sand on which to sit the pool, raising the shallow end up to the correct level by means of a temporary support of bricks. The top edge of the pool should be about 1 inch (2.5 cm) below the surrounding ground level; this ensures that when backfilling takes place. the lifting of the pool, which is inevitable, leaves it at ground level and not above.

3. Fill in all around the pool. Throughout backfilling it is vital to ensure that the pool is level from side to side and end to end. This can be readily checked with a length of board stood on edge from one side to the other with a spirit level placed in the middle. When the garden soil is in good condition it is possible to backfill with that. However, it is much easier to use a consistent medium like sand or pea gravel, which have the advantage of flowing easily and eliminating any air pockets. This should be firmly rammed to ensure that the pool is well seated.

4. Water can then be added. In the case of the plastic kinds it is useful to add water as the backfilling is done. so that there is a degree of rigidity. Providing that the levels are correct at the outset and water is run into the pool at the same rate as backfilling takes place there is unlikely to be any problem. Being non-toxic the pool can be planted straightaway.

5. The Concrete Pool

Although really hard work to construct, a concrete pool that is properly installed is the basis of the most successful water garden. Not only can almost any fanciful shape be built, but it is durable and after a couple of seasons begins to look completely natural. It is vital at the outset to bear in mind the limitations placed upon the project by the nature of the materials used, for although almost any shape can be moulded in concrete, it is more sensible to create an excavation that can be simply constructed.

Building the pool

1. The excavation must allow for the thickness of the concrete and should therefore be at least 6 ins (15 cm) larger than the finished pool, the sides and floor being rammed and firmed before concreting takes place. Sloping walls that require no shuttering are preferable to sheer sides that demand a complicated tangle of boards and supports. So that the concrete does not dry out too quickly it is a good idea to line the entire excavation with builders polythene before commencing.

2. Ideally concreting should be undertaken in a single day. Certainly no more than 24 hours should be allowed to elapse between joining two areas of concrete or else a potential point of weakness will be created. When a joint has to be made, the surface of the previous day's concrete should have been 'roughed up' to allow the new batch to key with it. Mixing concrete is hard work, but there is nothing mysterious about it. A suitable mixture consists of one part cement, two parts sand and four parts $\frac{3}{4}$ inch (2 cm) gravel measured out with a shovel or bucket. This is mixed dry until of a uniform greyish colour. When a waterproofing compound is to be added it is done at this stage. There are a number of different kinds available in a readily dispensed powder form. Water is added to the mixture until it is wet and stiff. A good test of its readiness is to place the shovel in the mixture and then withdraw it in a series of jerks. If the

ridges that this produces retain their character then the concrete is ready to be laid.

3. The first layer should be spread to a depth of 4 ins (10 cm) over the entire excavation. Large mesh wire netting like that used by poultry farmers is then pressed into the wet concrete to act as reinforcement. A further 2 ins (5 cm) of concrete is spread over this. The final layer should be carefully smoothed out with a plasterer's trowel. When the sides are steep, formwork or shuttering has to be erected and the concrete poured behind this. Usually of wooden construction, it is vital to paint the surface of the shuttering boards with limewash to ensure that the concrete does not stick and pull away when they are removed. In some cases, merely soaking the timber with water overcomes the problem of concrete and wood uniting.

4. When the concrete has been laid, and after any lingering surface moisture has soaked away, the surface of the concrete should be covered in wet sacks or something similar. Rapid drying out of the surface causes hair cracks to appear and these are potential areas of weaknesses. If the concrete surface area is so large that it is totally impracticable to cover it with sacks, then a gentle sprinkling of water from a can with a fine rose will provide a suitable alternative. It depends upon subsequent weather conditions, but after a week the concrete should have 'gone off' sufficiently to allow it to be treated with a sealant.

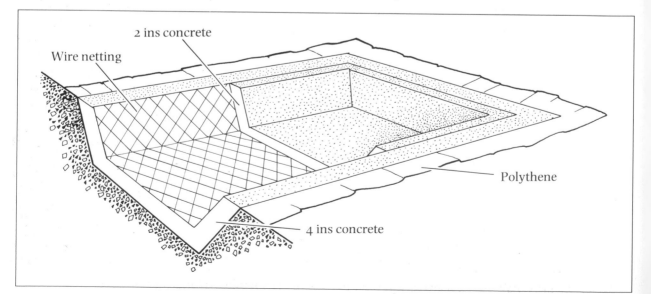

2 ins concrete

Wire netting

Polythene

4 ins concrete

Treating the concrete

Most gardeners will be aware that concrete contains free lime which is injurious to fish and plants in varying degrees. An untreated pool that is filled with water will immediately turn milky and be a most hostile environment for aquatic life. The constant filling and emptying of a newly constructed pool will eventually bring about its reduction, but treatment with a suitable sealant will be permanent. When the concrete is thoroughly dry a product such as Silglaze can be painted on to the surface. This neutralises the lime and by a complex reaction forms a silica which seals the concrete by internal glazing. Rubber-based and liquid-plastic paints are also useful in preventing free lime from escaping, although their principal role is as a waterproof pond sealant. These paints are available in a range of colours and provide an excellent finish to the concrete pool, but it is important not to neglect the need for a primer. Without this, the entire paint surface will become detached from the concrete like an enormous pool liner. Special primers for these paints are frequently available from garden centres. Being of a clear syrupy liquid they are easily and quickly applied with a brush, but you must ensure that every exposed concrete area is treated. Once protected against the effects of free lime, planting can take place immediately.

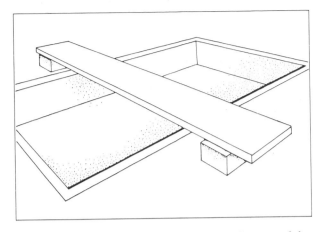

Raised planks will enable you to reach all parts of the pool.

This elegant and simple formal pool has a paved surround on which tubs of plants are displayed.

6. Tub and Sink Gardens

Any small container that is capable of holding water is a potential water garden. Old galvanised water tanks, sinks and baths with their outlets plugged up with putty are all extremely serviceable when sunk in the ground. Metal containers though, will eventually corrode and leak unless protected initially by a good coat of rubber-based paint. Old wine and vinegar casks can be turned into excellent small pools when sawn in half, but tubs that have contained oils, tar or wood preservatives should be avoided as any residue that remains is likely to pollute the water, forming an unsightly scum on the surface.

Before attempting to plant anything in the container it must be thoroughly scrubbed inside with clear water and then carefully rinsed out. On no account should detergent be used for cleaning as it is difficult to be sure when all traces have been removed. In tanks or sinks where algae or slimes have become established the addition of enough potassium permanganate to turn the water a violet colour will aid its removal.

Planting the container

When the selected container is absolutely clean, about 3 ins (8 cm) of good clean garden soil should be spread over the bottom. Avoid old leaves, pieces of turf or weeds in the compost as these will decompose and eventually pollute the water. So will soil that has been recently dressed with an artificial fertilizer, the abundance of mineral salts present creating a persistent algal bloom which is impossible to clear until all the fertilizer has been exhausted. The soil should be mixed into a muddy consistency by the addition of water and the miniature water garden will be ready for planting.

This can be done at any time during spring or early summer, choosing a miniature waterlily such as the yellow-flowered *Nymphaea pygmaea* 'Helvola' or its white cousin *N. pygmaea* 'Alba' as a centre piece. Alternatively the diminutive form of the brandy bottle or yellow pondlily, *Nuphar minimum*, can be exploited. Around the edge *Typha minima*, an attractive miniature form of the familiar 'bulrush' or reedmace with tiny brown poker heads can be planted together with the slender powder-blue *Mimulus ringens*. The water forget-me-not, cotton grass, bog arum and water

Cross-section of a planted tub

mint may also be tried, although the latter may need controlling towards the end of the season. Several bunches of one of the less vigorous kinds of submerged oxygenating plants like willow moss, starwort or tillaea can be introduced to help keep the water clear, although in a small volume of water with widely fluctuating temperatures this is not always easy.

After planting, but before water is added, the entire exposed soil surface should be covered with a generous layer of pea shingle to prevent fish from stirring up the soil in their quest for aquatic insect larvae. The end of the hosepipe used for filling the pool can be placed in a polythene bag on the bottom of the pool and the water switched on. By using the polythene bag in this way any turbulence that is likely to disturb the soil and gravel is avoided and the water remains nice and clear. The bag is removed with the hosepipe when the required level has been reached.

A couple of portions of floating plants like fairy moss or frogbit, half a dozen ramshorn snails and two or three small goldfish are added and the miniature water garden is complete. Routine maintenance is exactly the same as for an ordinary garden pond, although it is advisable to take the fish indoors for the winter months. Their survival would seem in doubt in a severe winter in such a small volume of water, but their presence in the summer is essential for the control of mosquito larvae.

Apart from using tubs and sinks for hardy aquatics, their use as temporary summer accommodation for half-hardy subjects should be considered. Some of the tropical waterlily cultivars flourish in such situations, together with the sacred lotus or nelumbo and old favourites like the water hyacinth and water poppy.

The same tub in full bloom

7. Fountains and Waterfalls

The movement of water in the garden adds a further dimension. Sounds and reflections which change constantly give a magical quality which appeals to all. Sadly, moving water and aquatic plants are not compatible and so arrangements should be made to grow water-dwelling plants as far away from water movement as possible. This aversion to moving water does not extend to the marginal subjects and these can be used freely in a pool of turbulent water. Certain underwater plants like water crowfoot and willow moss also show a degree of tolerance, but plants with floating leaves like waterlilies will rapidly deteriorate.

Moving water can take the form of a fountain or waterfall, or with modern pumps a combination of both. Pre-formed cascade and waterfall units are available and easily installed, and with the judicious use of pump outfalls can be a gentle tumbling stream or crashing, frothing waterfall. Their installation merely requires them to be seated squarely and evenly on the supporting soil. Fountains are easily contrived by attaching a suitable jet to the pump outlet. Ambitious gardeners can also compete with the grandest gardens in the land by incorporating an ornament with their fountain. Mermaids, nymphs and lions in imitation stone or lead are readily available with fittings which are compatible with most pumps. Those who have limited space need not be denied the pleasure of moving water as it is perfectly simple to attach a mask or gargoyle to a wall and connect fitments which permit it to spout water into a semi-circular pool below.

Choosing a pump

The choice of a suitable pump for the proposed fountain or waterfall should not be undertaken lightly. Most modern pumps designed for the garden pool are of strong manufacture, but their capacities vary widely and consequently the kind of effect that they can provide. There is nothing worse than a half-hearted fountain bouncing about in a murky pool, nor quite so irritating as a waterfall that does not have a continuous broad sheet of water passing over it. Most standard cascade units produced by fibreglass manufacturers require an output of at least 250 gallons (1140 litres) of water per hour to put a thin sheet of water across their width, while 300 gallons (1365 litres) per hour is necessary to make a continuous flow 6 ins (15 cm) wide. It can be somewhat difficult to assess visually the amount of water required for a given waterfall, but if a hose is run over the feature for one minute and the water collected in a container, the amount gathered measured in pints and multiplied by 7.5 will indicate the gallonage per hour.

There are two kinds of pumps popularly recommended for the garden pool; the submersible kind and the surface type. The latter is of little concern to the gardener with a small pool unless he wants to raise a high head of water. Installation is in a purpose-built, dry, weather-proof chamber for which expert assistance should be sought. For most pool owners submersible pumps are perfectly adequate. These are

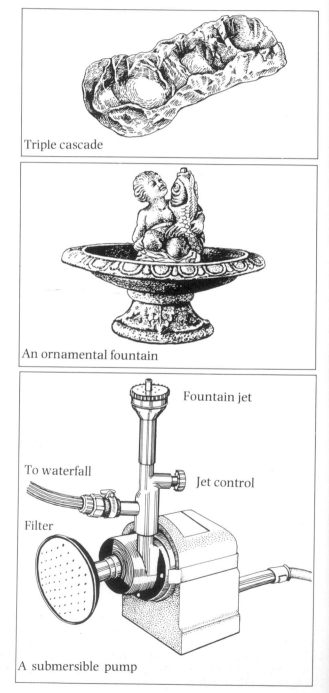

Triple cascade

An ornamental fountain

Fountain jet

To waterfall

Jet control

Filter

A submersible pump

the kind that are placed on the floor of the pool and through which water is drawn and pumped to a fountain or waterfall. They usually consist of a cast body containing a motor to which an input unit is attached which draws water into the pump, often through a strainer which catches any debris or filamentous algae likely to cause trouble within the unit. Above the input is the adjuster assembly which may comprise either a single or double outflow to allow water to be discharged as both fountain and waterfall. Control of water flow is by means of a simple adjuster screw. A fountain unit will have a jet with a series of holes in it that give a regular spray pattern. These are adjustable and removable so that the spray pattern and height can be altered to suit personal whim. When a waterfall is wanted a length of hose is attached which is sufficient to reach from the outflow to the head of the cascade unit.

There are no complications with installing a submersible pump. All that is required is a level surface within the pool on which to stand the pump unit and sufficient waterproof cable to reach the electricity supply. A length of cable will already be attached to the pump, often with a cable connector. It is convenient if the connection to the main cable from the house can be made beneath a paving slab near the pool; apart from providing protection for the connector, it allows you during the winter to disconnect and remove the pump and use the electrical point for the attachment of a pool heater.

Attaching a filter

While the majority of submersible pumps have filters as part of their input assembly to prevent debris from interfering with the flow, it is quite possible to fit filters that will remove free-floating water-discolouring algae which make the pool look so unsightly. These should not be used as a substitute for a healthy balance within the pool, but in certain circumstances, especially in the early days of the pool's life, they can perform an invaluable role. Most look merely like a deep tray, but there are in fact two trays, one inside the other. The inner one will contain a foam filter element which is covered with a generous layer of charcoal or gravel. The pump is connected to the outer tray and draws water in through the charcoal or gravel and then through the filter element into the pump for subsequent discharge. Algae and other organic debris collect in the medium in the middle tray which is regularly changed.

The ambitious gardener can further enhance the beauty of his fountain or waterfall by the addition of underwater lighting. Strategically placed, this can either highlight a feature or illuminate the entire pool. Specially manufactured spotlights are readily available, these being encased in sealed alloy underwater lampholder units. They are available with a choice of colour lenses to give a single colour illumination, although one enterprising manufacturer has developed a rotating colour changer which can be adjusted to give slow or rapid changes of several colours.

8. Creating a Balance

When constructing and stocking a water garden feature, the gardener is creating a totally different environment in which plants and livestock depend totally upon one another for their continued existence. This of course happens in the garden, but an individual garden is only part of the great outdoors, whereas the garden pool is a complete miniature environment in itself. With the creation of a natural balance comes healthy water conditions, the desire of every pool owner.

The benefits of plants

One of the biggest misconceptions in water gardening is that if the pool is well oxygenated it will always remain clear. Thus if one introduces a fountain to the pool it should be a magical cure-all, for the droplets falling into the pool pick up oxygen on the way down. The fact that the droplets are well oxygenated is not in dispute, and on warm sultry days the fish will delight in their cool spray, but the presence of oxygen is no guarantee of clarity. The misunderstanding has been inadvertently created by the fact that it is submerged oxygenating plants which have the greatest influence on the state of the water. However, it is not the oxygen that the plants produce that does the trick, but the competition that they provide for the green, water-discolouring algae which invade the pool as soon as it is warmed by spring sunshine. These primitive forms of plant life flourish in water that is rich in mineral salts, and it is only when competition is provided by higher plants for these mineral salts that there is any chance of them coming under control. Obviously if there is sufficient underwater plant growth to use the mineral salts that are present, then the water will be clear. Only when there is an abundance of plant foods available will algae and submerged plants live alongside one another. This points to the importance of using fertilisers carefully so that minimal quantities become freely available in the water.

Shade also helps to reduce the occurrence of algae – obviously not shade that is going to prevent the successful and vigorous growth of aquatic plants, but that which prevents sunlight from penetrating the water. It is undesirable that the entire surface of the water be covered with foliage on practical and aesthetic grounds, but for a reasonably even balance to be achieved from the beginning, at least a third of the surface area should be covered either with the floating foliage of waterlilies or free-floating aquatic plants. In assessing the area to be covered, ignore that occupied by the shallows and then permit one third of the remainder to become colonised. Similarly, when calculating the number of submerged oxygenating plants to be included, allow one bunch for every square foot of surface area. That is not to say that the bunches of plants need to be distributed evenly over the pool floor; it is just the quantity required for the given surface area. Most submerged oxygenating plants are sold as bunches of cuttings fastened together with a lead weight and it is upon this typical plant material that the calculation is based.

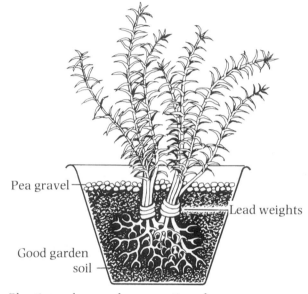

Pea gravel

Lead weights

Good garden soil

Planting submerged oxygenating plants

Starworts

The benefits of fish

Submerged oxygenating plants are required by fish as a source of oxygen and, when fine-leafed kinds are grown, as a suitable place for the deposition of spawn. Floating leaves provide shelter and a respite from the hot summer sun. Certain plants like the starworts also provide green matter, an essential part of the diet of all coldwater fish; while the fish reciprocate by depositing organic matter rich in plant foods and controlling many aquatic insect pests. The gardener also depends upon fish for the control of mosquito larvae, inevitable inhabitants of the garden pool and tiresome progeny of the gardener's foe. As with the plants, the fish are introduced in such numbers as will create harmony. Using the same calculation, allow 2 ins (5 cm) of fish to every square foot of surface area. This allows for development, growth and breeding. A maximum of 6 ins (15 cm) length of fish can be achieved eventually, but beyond this casualties will occur as the pool becomes unbalanced. The calculation of the length of fish is based upon the distance from nose to tail. Thus one can have many small fish, a few large fish or a moderate number of each.

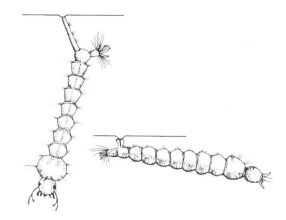

Mosquito larvae × 8

Other pond life

Other livestock can be introduced freely and indeed frogs and toads will doubtless make their own way to the pool. Snails of the ramshorn kind graze upon algae and assist in its control. They also reproduce freely, but seldom over-populate the pool as fish regard their eggs as a delicacy. Freshwater mussels help in the control of free-floating algae by acting as a siphon, drawing algae-laden water in and blowing clear water out. Their introduction into a new pool is fraught with difficulty as they dislike such a sterile environment. In the mellow waters of an established pool they are quite at home, but it would be unwise to introduce more than two or three to the average pond.

This is not the case with marginal plants, which we have so far ignored, for of all the components of a happy balance this is the one that has the least influence. Marginal plants in all their diversity can be planted freely, although on aesthetic grounds it is better not to overdo them.

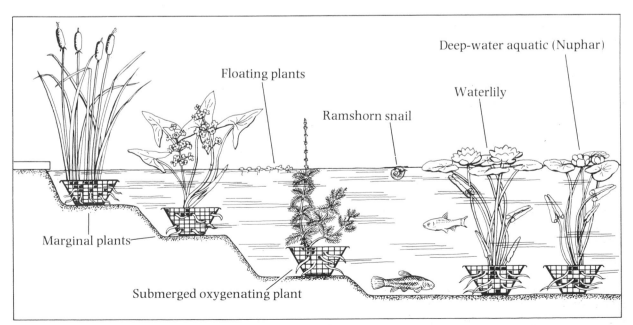

Floating plants

Deep-water aquatic (Nuphar)

Waterlily

Ramshorn snail

Marginal plants

Submerged oxygenating plant

A balanced pool

9. Deep-water Aquatics

Waterlilies are obviously the most widely grown deep-water aquatics. But apart from these great beauties there are a number of other very worthy aquatics that will happily flourish in deeper water. None has the startling brilliance of the nymphaeas, but some will tolerate conditions which the waterlilies would abhor.

Aponogeton distachyus Water Hawthorn. Although a native of South Africa and having a somewhat tropical appearance, this little fellow is reliably hardy and provides blossoms for probably the longest period of all. In mild areas it will start flowering during late April and will continue until the first sharp frost, usually in November. The individual flowers are forked into two arms and bear a double row of bract-like organs at the base of which are clusters of jet-black stamens. This gives a most striking effect which, coupled with its cloying vanilla fragrance, makes it a most desirable inhabitant of the smaller pool. It has small more or less oblong or oval green leaves with dark maroon blotches. These form a group up to $1\frac{1}{2}$ ft (45 cm) across, or a little more when grown in very deep water. The water hawthorn is happiest in between 1 ft (30 cm) and 3 ft (90 cm) of water, although it will tolerate as much as 5 ft (1.5 m). Propagation is occasionally by division of the tuber-like rootstock, or more frequently from seed. Seedlings often appear amongst marginal plants in shallows at the poolside.

Aponogeton distachyus (Water Hawthorn)

Brasenia schreberi Water Shield or Water Target. Very few nurserymen regularly stock this waterlily-like aquatic, but it seems to be one that will soon become more readily available. It certainly deserves to, for its fleshy rounded floating leaves and bright purple three- or four-petalled floating flowers are of a most distinctive and attractive appearance. Small boys are also enthralled by the curious seed pods which follow, each containing one or two seeds that are dispersed through a removable lid on top of each pod. Brasenia is a little more difficult to cultivate than most deep-water aquatics, but the results are worthwhile. It requires acid water that is no deeper than 2–3 ft (60–90 cm) and can be readily increased from seed sown immediately in a tray of mud.

Nuphar Spatterdocks or Pondlilies. This is a group of plants that often causes confusion, for in their early life, nuphars look very much like nymphaeas and being popularly called pondlilies adds to the confusion. While not wishing to be disparaging about the nuphars, it has to be said that in no way can they compare with nymphaeas for grace, elegance and beauty. Their leaves are more rank and vigorous, while their flowers are scarcely significant. Unlike the true waterlilies though, the pondlilies are tolerant of a certain amount of shade and are not concerned about moving water. It is only when these conditions prevail that it can be considered prudent to replace nymphaeas with nuphars. It is possible to raise the species from seed, but propagation by the division of the root-stocks and taking of eyes, as recommended for waterlilies, is much quicker and simpler.

N. advenum American Spatterdock or Mooseroot. A bold vigorous species with large green leathery leaves and translucent, ruffled and frilled, submerged foliage. Even when given adequate room this species is likely to produce upright aerial foliage from the centre of the crown. Globular yellow flowers tinged with purple, orange stamens. Prefers over 3 ft (90 cm) depth of water.

N. lutea Yellow Pondlily or Brandy Bottle. A common native species often seen in farm ponds and quiet waterways. Large leathery green floating leaves, crimpled transluscent submerged foliage and small globular yellow flowers with a strong alcoholic odour. There are a number of different forms of this with varying leaf shapes and flower colouration which are sometimes offered by aquatics specialists. Requires at least 3 ft (90 cm) of water before giving of its best.

N. minimum Dwarf Pond Lily. There is a lot of confusion as to whether this is the same as *N. pumila*. While the botanists agree or disagree, whatever the name it is virtually the same plant to the gardener. An attractive dwarf for the rock pool or sink garden with tiny pale yellow blooms amongst handsome small heart-shaped leaves. It will prosper in between $1-1\frac{1}{2}$ ft (30–40 cm) of water.

N. polysepalum. One of the better nuphars for shallow areas. It will tolerate as little as 1 ft (30 cm) of water or as much as 3 ft (90 cm). The floating leaves are lance-shaped and sprinkled with small golden-yellow goblet-like blossoms.

N. rubrodiscum Red Disced Pond Lily. A moderate grower requiring about 3 ft (90 cm) of water. It has long floating leathery leaves, which are occasionally erect, and most attractive underwater foliage. The large rounded yellow blossoms have bright crimson central stigmatic discs.

N. sagittifolium Cape Fear Spatterdock. While not generally recommended for pool culture, this frequent inhabitant of coldwater aquaria can make a useful contribution to the pool. In most parts of the country it is hardy, sporting soft yellow flowers followed by marble-like fruits amongst acutely cut glossy green foliage. Prefers no more than $1\frac{1}{2}$ ft (45 cm) of water.

Nymphoides peltata (syn. **Villarsia nymphoides**) Water Fringe. This charming little aquatic masquerades equally under each Latin name. However, no matter what it is called it is an aquatic of merit, flourishing in up to $2\frac{1}{2}$ ft (75 cm) of water or as little as 9 ins (23 cm). During late summer it lightens the pool with a wonderful display of delicate yellow fringed buttercup-like flowers amidst handsome green and brown mottled foliage reminiscent of a pygmy waterlily. Surprisingly a relative of the gentians of alpine regions, it rapidly colonises its allotted space with a wiry creeping rootstock. This can be divided during the summer and forms an easy means of propagation.

Orontium aquaticum Golden Club. Probably the most adaptable deep water aquatic, for it is equally tolerant of wet muddy conditions. For this reason it is an ideal inhabitant of ditch or stream gardens where the water level is never constant. It is a rather extraordinary member of the arum family which makes a striking display of golden and white pencil-like flowers during April and May, which emerge from the water and stand to attention amongst waxy glaucous foliage. It is not an easy plant to divide and generally resents disturbance. Seed is the usual means of propagation, but this must be gathered fresh and sown immediately in pans of mud.

Nuphar lutea (Yellow Pondlily or Brandy Bottle)

10. Waterlilies

Waterlilies are the much-loved queens of the water garden, flaunting gorgeous waxy blossoms of white, red, pink or yellow amongst verdant floating foliage. The true waterlilies are known botanically as *Nymphaea*. Pondlilies are the less desirable, small-flowered *Nuphar*.

Waterlilies in common with other aquatic plants are best planted between the months of April and August. When planted during April or May a reasonable display can be expected the first summer.

Choosing a container

The container that is used for a waterlily must be carefully selected. Properly designed aquatic planting baskets are available and these fulfil the purpose admirably. They are usually made of tough plastic, with lattice-work sides and a broad base to give them stability. The open sides are essential for successful waterlily culture. If planted in pots or solid-sided containers waterlilies deteriorate quickly, becoming dwarfed, sickly and flowering sparingly. Occasionally wooden planting crates become available and these are equally suitable.

Some pool owners prefer to plant their waterlilies directly into soil on the pool floor. While satisfactory growth will result, the maintenance of such plants is fraught with difficulty, the stronger varieties rapidly swamping their weaker neighbours. Only in a natural pool should direct planting be contemplated.

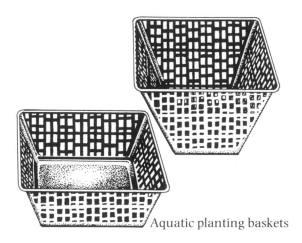

Aquatic planting baskets

Preparing the plant

As waterlilies are planted during their active growing period, they are likely to have an excess of root and foliage which may hinder their establishment. Hardy waterlilies have rootstocks of one of two kinds; both are stout and fleshy. The most frequently encountered is vertical and log-like with a bold tuft of vigorous foliage on the top and a ruff of fibrous roots immediately beneath. The other is generally thinner, horizontal, and with the growing point at one end. In both cases growth is made from one extremity of the rootstock, so that the non-growing end is older and often showing signs of deterioration. To ensure that any premature rotting of the rootstock is arrested, it is advisable to pare the end of the fleshy rootstock with a sharp knife to expose healthy tissue and then dust the wound with powdered charcoal or flowers of sulphur to prevent infection. Apart from the small, vigorous, spear-like shoots which arise from the growing point, all other foliage should be removed. In most cases it dies anyway, and if it does not then it gives the plant buoyancy and lifts it right out of the basket.

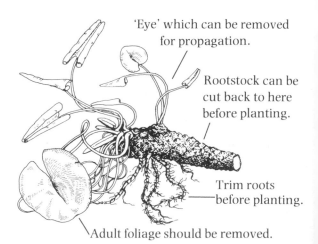

'Eye' which can be removed for propagation.

Rootstock can be cut back to here before planting.

Trim roots before planting.

Adult foliage should be removed.

Soil preparation

Fortunately nowadays we understand a little more about the waterlily's requirements, which are quite simply good heavy garden soil. This should not be gathered from the vegetable plot as this is likely to have been dressed with an artificial fertiliser, which if introduced to the pool will pollute the water. Any organic matter such as twigs, weeds, leaves or pieces of turf should likewise be avoided as they too will cause problems during their decomposition. If it is felt that the soil requires extra fertiliser, then the addition of a liberal dressing of coarse bonemeal is beneficial and will cause minimal pollution.

Planting a waterlily

The container should be filled with prepared soil to within 1 in (2.5 cm) of the top. If the soil is very light and likely to pass through the holes in the sides of the container, then the basket can be lined with hessian before being filled with soil. The waterlily is then planted in the centre of the basket, given a further light dressing of soil and thoroughly soaked with water from a watering can with a fine rose. This drives out all the air and prevents debris from being expelled into the water. It also allows any subsidence to be made good before the final top dressing of washed pea shingle. This helps prevent soil polluting the water and also makes it impossible for adventurous fish to stir up the mud in their quest for aquatic insect larvae.

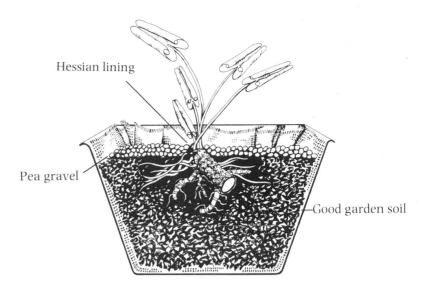

Hessian lining

Pea gravel

Good garden soil

When a natural pool requires planting and the waterlilies are going to grow directly on the pool floor, then the plants merely need wrapping in a hessian package containing some good quality soil, their noses just protruding, and gently lowering into position.

Waterlilies are naturally plants of quiet backwaters and resent constantly moving water, so if a fountain or waterfall is envisaged, it is important that the waterlilies are kept as far away as possible.

Placing in the pool

While it is not recommended to leave foliage on newly planted waterlilies, many gardeners do so in the vain hope that they will create an instant effect. As waterlily leaves are essentially floating, it is important not to 'drown' them, so plants with leaves need raising up on bricks in the pool so that the leaves float on the surface of the water. As the leaf stalks lengthen, the plants can be gradually lowered.

When all the foliage has been removed the baskets can be lowered to their permanent positions without any trouble. The simplest way of lowering baskets is with assistance. Two lengths of strong string or binder twine are passed through the upper holes in the basket. The strings should run parallel to one another and act as handles so that one person can stand on each side of the pool and gently lower the basket to the floor. The strings are quite easily withdrawn.

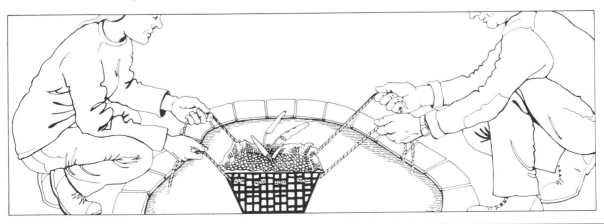

When given the correct depth of water and full uninterrupted daylight, waterlilies will provide a dazzling display of colour from June until the first sharp frost of autumn. They are long-lived, require little attention, and so are invaluable to the modern gardener.

A close watch should be kept for the predations of waterlily aphids and other pests and diseases (see pages 58–59). These can all be controlled with a fair degree of success if caught in their early stages.

Feeding

As with most other plants growing in pots or containers, feeding is a necessity. Specific waterlily fertilisers are available, usually in small individual sachets which have their perforations exposed and are then pushed into the soil alongside the waterlily. This follows the older, but equally useful method of making balls of clay or heavy soil mixed with coarse bonemeal and then pushing them into the soil next to the plant. These bonemeal 'pills' are easily contrived and most effective.

Dividing

Every few years waterlilies benefit from being lifted and divided in much the same way as hardy herbaceous plants. The need for this becomes evident when a basket becomes congested, leaf size diminishes, flowering is sporadic and the foliage in the centre of the plant starts to climb out of the water. All that is necessary is for the waterlily to be removed from its basket, the strongest growth selected and removed, and then replanted in fresh soil. Ideally this should be done during April or May.

Nymphaea laydekeri 'Alba'

Choosing varieties

Hardy waterlilies occur in every expected colour except blue and in varieties that will grow in as little as 6 ins (15 cm) of water in a sink garden or as much as 10 ft (3 m) in a lake. There is a reasonable latitude regarding the depths of water at which individual waterlilies will flourish, but it is important to select smaller kinds for the modern pool, rather than try to force vigorous popular kinds into depths at which they will not develop properly.

Pygmy waterlilies (Up to 1 ft (30 cm) of water)

Nymphaea pygmaea 'Alba' The smallest white waterlily with flowers no more than 1 in (25 mm) across and miniature, dark green, oval leaves.
Nymphaea pygmaea 'Helvola' Bright canary-yellow flowers with orange stamens are produced amongst small, olive-green foliage heavily mottled with maroon and brown.
Nymphaea pygmaea 'Rubra' Tiny, bright red flowers and purplish-green leaves. Not as free-flowering as the preceding two.

Small-growing waterlilies (Up to 2 ft (60 cm) of water)

Nymphaea laydekeri 'Alba' Pure white blossoms with yellow stamens noted for their distinctive aroma reminiscent of a freshly-opened packet of tea.
Nymphaea laydekeri 'Fulgens' Bright crimson, fragrant flowers with reddish stamens. Dark green leaves with deep purplish undersides.
Nymphaea laydekeri 'Purpurata' Splendid vinous-red blossoms with bright orange stamens. Small, dark green leaves sometimes splashed with maroon.
Nymphaea odorata 'Sulphurea Grandiflora' Fragrant, canary-yellow, star-shaped blooms and distinctive, dark green foliage mottled with purple and brown.
Nymphaea 'Graziella' Striking orange-red flowers with deep orange stamens float amongst olive-green leaves splashed and stained with purple and brown.
Nymphaea 'Sioux' Attractive, pale yellow blossoms pass through orange to crimson. Dark olive-green foliage mottled with purple.

Nymphaea 'James Brydon'

Medium-growing waterlilies (Up to 3 ft (90 cm) of water)

Nymphaea marliacea 'Albida' Pure white, fragrant blossoms held just above the large, apple-green leaves.
Nymphaea marliacea 'Carnea' Large, flesh-pink, star-shaped blossoms with golden stamens. The flowers on newly established plants often open white for the first few months. Large, deep green leaves.
Nymphaea marliacea 'Chromatella' Rich yellow flowers with golden stamens are produced amongst olive-green leaves which are heavily spotted with maroon and bronze.
Nymphaea marliacea 'Flammea' Bright red flowers flecked with white. The outer petals are deep pink and the deep olive-green leaves heavily mottled with brown and maroon.
Nymphaea 'Alaska' A recent introduction with huge white flowers and a dense cluster of yellow stamens.
Nymphaea 'Gonnere' Pure white double blossoms like snowballs bob about amongst luxuriant, pea-green foliage.
Nymphaea 'James Brydon' Large, fragrant, paeony-shaped flowers float amongst dark purplish-green leaves that are occasionally flecked with maroon. See above.
Nymphaea 'Louise' A recent introduction with deep red, fully double, cup-shaped blossoms. Each individual petal is tipped with white.
Nymphaea 'Mrs. Richmond' Pale rose-pink flowers which pass to crimson with age rest amongst fresh green foliage.
Nymphaea 'Rose Arey' One of the loveliest pink varieties with star-shaped blossoms that produce a delicious aniseed fragrance. The juvenile foliage is crimson, but changes to green as it matures.
Nymphaea 'Sunrise' The most fragrant yellow variety with large, soft canary blossoms amongst dull green foliage which is occasionally flecked with brown.
Nymphaea 'Virginalis' Pure icy-white, semi-double blossoms with bright yellow stamens arise from amongst handsome, green foliage with a purplish flush.

Vigorous-growing waterlilies (Over 3 ft (90 cm) of water)

Nymphaea 'Attraction' Large, garnet-red flowers flecked with white up to 9 ins (23 cm) across when fully open. Immense, dark green leaves.
Nymphaea 'Charles de Meurville' Plum-coloured blossoms tipped and streaked with white. Handsome olive-green foliage.
Nymphaea 'Gladstoniana' Huge, waxy, white blossoms like immense floating soup dishes amongst large, dark green leaves.

11. Marginal Plants

Marginal plants may best be described as those aquatics which grow in wet mud or shallow water towards the edge of the pool. Treatment is much the same as for waterlilies, except that instead of being planted in baskets, they are not infrequently established directly into soil that has been spread along the marginal shelf. Planting in groups of two or three of the same kind is preferable giving a more pleasing and natural effect.

Acorus calamus Sweet Flag. An iris-like aquatic which is surprisingly a member of the arum family. The leaves are bright green and sword-shaped with a strong tangerine fragrance. Strange little greenish horn-like flowers are produced during the summer. There is a lovely variegated foliage variety called 'Variegatus'. This has leaves that are boldly banded with cream and green, suffused with rose in early spring. Increased by division. 3 ft (90 cm).

A. gramineus A much shorter species with fine grassy foliage of similar character. Excellent for the rock pool of sink garden. An excellent variegated form is sometimes available from nurserymen. Increased by division. 10 ins (25 cm).

Alisma parviflora This North American version of the water plantain has distinct rounded leaves and short pyramids of pink and white flowers. Ideal for the smaller pool. Easily raised from seed. $1\frac{1}{2}$ ft (75 cm).

A. plantago-aquatica Water Plantain. Familiar in pools and streams in many parts of Britain, this handsome aquatic should be introduced to the garden pool with a certain amount of reserve. If not carefully controlled it will get out of hand, so immediately the loose pyramidal panicles of pink and white blossoms have faded the old flower spike should be removed. The quantity of viable seed scattered by a single flower spike is quite remarkable. The foliage is ovate, glossy green, and held boldly out of the water. 1–3 ft (30–90 cm).

Baldellia ranunculoides Floating or Lesser Water Plantain. Formerly known as *Alisma ranunculoides* (a name to which it still answers in the nursery trade), this smaller version of the popular water plantains has tiny floating leaves and distinctive solitary white flowers with a bright yellow blotch. Unlike the alismas it needs to be constantly immersed and is therefore of little use in a pool where the water level fluctuates widely.

Butomus umbellatus Flowering Rush. At first glance this could be taken to be another of the very mediocre rushes that populate garden pools up and down the country. This assumption is soon dispelled when, in late summer, umbels of striking rose-pink blossoms are produced. $2\frac{1}{2}$ ft (75 cm).

Calla palustris Bog Arum. A creeping plant that can be used to great effect in masking the edge of the pool. It has glossy green heart-shaped leaves from amongst which small white arum-like flowers appear. Most years these are followed by red berries which provide a source of seed for propagation. Otherwise this plant is increased by cutting up sections of creeping stem which root into the mud. 8 ins (20 cm).

Acorus calamus

Alisma plantago-aquatica

Calla palustris

Caltha leptosepala Mountain Marigold. This is the best of the white-flowered marsh marigolds with glistening silvery-white blossoms in spring and handsome dark green scalloped leaves. Can be raised from seed or division. 1 ft 4 ins (40 cm).

C. palustris Marsh Marigold, Kingcup. An ever popular native spring-flowering subject for pool or waterside, tolerant of a wide variety of conditions, but delighting the gardener with its rich golden flowers above bold mounds of dark green foliage. The white form *alba* has little to recommend it as it seems particularly prone to mildew. The gorgeous double 'Flore Pleno' is a must for every water garden, with neat hummocks of foliage and bright yellow button-like flowers rather like those of pompon dahlia. Both can be increased by division and the species from freshly sown seed as well. 1 ft (30 cm).

Carex pendula Pendulous Sedge. A lovely native of wet meadows and woodland fringes which is quite at home in the water garden. Although enjoying wet conditions it will seldom prosper in more than 4 ins (10 cm) of water. With graceful grass-like foliage it adds a pleasant green foil to the waterside and is further enhanced during the late summer by long brownish catkin-like flowers. Easily increased from seed. 3 ft (90 cm).

C. riparia Great Pond Sedge. Not a suitable plant for the average pool as it is rather coarse and invasive, but its cultivars 'Aurea' with bright golden leaves and 'Variegata' with green and white striped foliage are well worth acquiring. Careful division is the best method of propagation. 2 ft (60 cm).

Cyperus longus Sweet Galingale. Those who know the florist's umbrella plant, *Cyperus alternifolius*, would have no difficulty in recognising this useful aquatic. It has tall grassy foliage arranged in a stiff spiky whorl like the ribs of an umbrella. During late summer these striking leaf arrangements are sprinkled with brownish flower spikelets. Increased by division of the creeping rootstock or seed sown shortly after it has been gathered. 3 ft (90 cm).

Eriophorum angustifolium Cotton Grass. Handsome grassy foliage with cotton wool-like seeding heads during early summer. Must have an acid soil. Increased by division. 1 ft (30 cm).

E. latifolium Another similar species which is sometimes offered by nurserymen, but which is much more difficult to establish. An acid-lover which can be propagated by careful division.

Glyceria aquatica 'Variegata' Variegated Water Grass. A superb perennial grass with cream and green striped foliage which is brightly flushed with deep rose-pink. Easily increased by division. 3 ft (90 cm).

Houttuynia cordata A strange but useful dwarf-growing plant with bluish-green heart-shaped leaves and white four-petalled flowers with hard central cones. In the beautiful fully double form 'Plena' the many petals disguise the prominent cone completely. A creeping plant with strong-smelling foliage it is ideal for disguising the harsh edge of an artificial pool. The creeping rootstock is easily divided. 1 ft (30 cm).

Hypericum elodes Surprisingly there is a creeping aquatic species of hypericum. Most species are shade lovers and prefer dryish conditions, but this little fellow scrambles about the poolside distributing its charming golden saucer-shaped blossoms amongst tiny soft green leaves during late summer. Cuttings root freely. 3–6 ins (8–15 cm).

Caltha palustris

Cyperus longus

Houttuynia cordata

Iris laevigata 'Snowdrift'

Iris versicolor 'Kermesina'

Hybrid Mimulus

Iris laevigata This is the true blue flowered iris of the Asian paddy fields, a much loved and welcome addition to the water garden. It flowers during June and early July with lovely sky-blue blossoms amongst clumps of sturdy upright foliage. There are innumerable cultivars available in a wide colour range. 'Monstrosa' is violet and white, 'Rose Queen' a soft pink and 'Alba', cool icy white. There is also a first class variegated foliage variety known variously as 'Variegata' and 'Elegantissima'. The common blue *Iris laevigata* can be increased by seed or division, but the named varieties must be propagated by division which should take place immediately after flowering. 3 ft (90 cm).

I. pseudacorus Yellow Flag. A tall coarse native which is only suitable for the large or natural pool, but which has produced a splendid short-growing variegated variety. Known as 'Variegata', this has brightly variegated leaves of gold and green. For those who have a liking for our native yellow flag, but cannot accommodate its bulk, the more refined 'Golden Queen' and soft primrose *bastardii* can be recommended. All the garden varieties should be increased by division after flowering. 2½–3 ft (75–90 cm).

I. versicolor This Northern American native with handsome violet blossoms veined with purple and splashed with gold deserves a place in any garden pool. Well restrained, it flowers throughout June and into July amongst rich green sword-like foliage. An even lovelier cultivar called 'Kermesina' is of similar habit, but with exquisite blooms of rich plum-purple. *Iris versicolor* is easily raised from seed, but 'Kermesina' must be divided after flowering. 2½ ft (75 cm).

Juncus effusus Soft Rush. This common and invasive native weed of ponds and streams throughout the British Isles has yielded two interesting and unusual cultivars for the keen gardener. *Juncus effusus* 'Spiralis' is a form with curiously twisted stems that grow in a corkscrew fashion and 'Vittatus', which is also known as 'Aureo-striatus', has stems some 2 ft (60 cm) high which are striped with green and yellow. As with many variegated plants, occasional green stems appear and these should be removed to prevent them from smothering the desirable striped foliage.

Ludwigia palustris False Loosestrife. Most ludwigias are aquarium plants, but this attractive native is more of a swamp or marginal plant with very fine green leaves that have a purplish cast. Its flowers are insignificant, which makes it a doubtful inhabitant of the small pool, but for the larger pool, stream or ditch it is invaluable. 1 ft (30 cm).

Mentha aquatica Water Mint. This is a strongly aromatic relative of our familiar garden mint which enjoys shallow water or mud at the pool side. It can be rather invasive if not dealt with sternly, but is quite manageable when confined to a proper planting basket. Throughout late summer it produces dense terminal whorls of lilac-pink flowers on slender reddish stems amongst a profusion of downy greyish-green foliage. It is easily increased by division, but young cuttings of emerging shoots taken during spring root readily in pans of mud. 1 ft (30 cm).

Menyanthes trifoliata Bog or Buck Bean. This is a sprawling, but well-behaved plant for shallow water, its trifoliate foliage being very reminiscent of a broad bean. The white-fringed flowers are produced during May above the dark green foliage. It is possible to grow the bog bean from seed, but the simplest method of propagation is cutting the creeping rhizomes into sections, each containing a bud, and placing these in a tray of mud. 8 ins–1 ft (20–30 cm).

Mimulus luteus Musk. A familiar yellow antirrhinum-like flower which has established itself along streamsides over much of Britain. Attaining a height of no more than 1 ft (30 cm) it is not truly a marginal plant, although it will grow well in a couple of inches of water. It is a parent, together with *M. guttatus* and *M. cupreus*, of myriad brightly coloured cultivars which all have a cheerful if short life in the pool margins. 'Bonfire' is vivid red, 'Monarch Strain', pastel shades and 'Queen's Prize' boldly spotted. For those with a small pool, the tiny 'Whitecroft Scarlet' is superb, forming spreading carpets of fire scarcely 4 ins (10 cm) high. All the foregoing are unpredictable in their winter survival, and while all can be raised from seed on an annual basis, a longer flowering season is assured if groups of overwintering rosettes of foliage are lifted and placed in trays of soil in a cold frame.

M. ringens There is no problem with the longevity of this delicate looking aquatic. It is intolerant of muddy conditions, revelling in several inches of water. A native of North America, it has branching stems clothed in narrow leaflets sprinkled with dainty lavender-blue blossoms throughout the summer. It can be grown easily from seed, but is also readily increased from short stem-cuttings taken during the summer and rooted in a pan of mud. $1\frac{1}{2}$ ft (45 cm).

Myosotis scorpioides Water Forget-me-not. This is very similar in appearance to our popular bedding forget-me-not, except that it flowers throughout the summer and is a reliable perennial. Frequently known as *M. palustris*, this little beauty forms neat hummocks of smooth light green leaves smothered in azure blossoms. There are white and pinkish forms available, together with an improved cultivar called 'Semperflorens'. This and the species are easily raised from seed sown in the spring, or from division of the clumps which become large and untidy if not periodically attended to. 8 ins (20 cm).

Narthecium ossifragum Bog Asphodel. A small plant for the small pool or sink garden which dislikes more than the barest covering of water. It is interesting rather than spectacular, with small fans of reddish-green iris-like foliage amidst which short racemes of bright yellow flowers are produced. It can be readily increased by seed or division of the clumps of foliage. 1 ft (30 cm).

Peltandra alba This is the white-spathed version of the arrow arum, *P. virginica*. In almost every way it is similar to that plant. $1\frac{1}{2}$ ft (45 cm).

P. virginica Arrow Arum. This is the commonest of a small family of arum-like aquatics with dark green arrow-shaped leaves and narrow spathes which may be green or white. In this species the spathes are green and arise from a short fleshy rootstock that readily divides to form new plants. Seed is sometimes produced and if this can be sown straightaway, will provide sturdy young plants for planting in spring. $1\frac{1}{2}$ ft (45 cm).

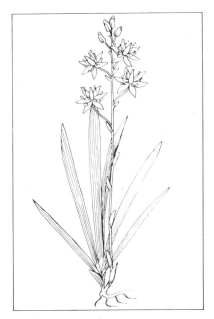

Narthecium ossifragum

This fine display of marginals includes a fair proportion of plants with bold foliage.

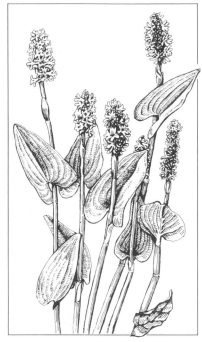

Pontederia cordata

Ranunculus lingua

Pontederia cordata Pickerel Weed. A splendid North American plant with bold spires of soft blue flowers amongst handsome ovate or lanceolate shiny green foliage. Growing no more than 3 ft (90 cm) high, it provides colour at the poolside throughout August and September. Propagation is easily effected by division of the rootstocks early in the spring when the fresh green shoots are just appearing. Seed can be sown, but must be green and fresh to have any chance of germinating.

Preslia cervina Although not widely available, this is one of the best aromatic plants for the poolside. It is easily increased from soft cuttings of young shoots taken during early spring and rooted in pans of wet mud. Of a neat, but spreading habit, it is ideal for hiding the harsh edges of the pool with its tangled, highly aromatic, lanceolate foliage. During late summer it is littered with stiff whorled spikes of dainty ultramarine or lilac blossoms. 1 ft (30 cm).

Ranunculus flammula Lesser Spearwort. Like a superior buttercup, this scrambling plant with dark oval green leaves and reddish stems forms dense colonies in shallow water. Except in the tiniest pool, it is not worth considering alone, but as an underplanting to a basket of tall-growing reeds or irises it cannot be faulted. Easily increased by cutting up pieces of creeping stem which root at every leaf joint. 8 ins–1 ft (20–30 cm).

R. lingua Greater Spearwort. This is the largest species of aquatic buttercup, with erect hollow stems that are clothed with narrow dark green or bluish-grey leaves. Large yellow buttercup-like flowers are produced for much of the summer. 'Grandiflora' is a variant which is larger and finer in all its parts. While seed of the species can be employed, propagation is easily effected in early spring by division and separation of the emerging shoots which appear in profusion from the creeping rootstock. 2–3 ft (60–90 cm).

Sagittaria japonica Japanese Arrowhead. This is closely related to our native arrowhead, *S. sagittifolia*, and is indeed described as such by some authorities. To the gardener they are quite distinct, the white blossoms of *S. japonica* having a bright golden centre, while those of *S. sagittifolia* are black and crimson. The foliage of the former is also less ridged and acutely arrow-shaped. Like most arrowheads, this grows from large rounded turions or winter buds which look rather like small potatoes. In some places these are known as duck potatoes, for ducks will forage for these in early spring just as the shoots are emerging. The turions give rise to handsome arrow-shaped foliage and spikes of pure white flowers with conspicuous centres. Those of the double 'Flore Pleno' are like tiny white powder-puffs. Propagation by lifting and separating the over-wintered turions just as they begin to sprout. 1½–2 ft (45–60 cm).

S. sagittifolia Arrowhead. Almost identical to the preceding, but with flowers that have black and crimson centres and leaves that are more ridged and acutely arrow-shaped. Flowers during the summer and rarely attains a height of more than 2 ft (60 cm).

Saururus cernuus Lizards' Tail. A rather strange, but attractive aquatic for shallow water with clumps of heart-shaped leaves which take on delightful autumnal tints. During July and August it sports nodding sprays of creamy-white flowers. Another saururus called *S. loureiri* has

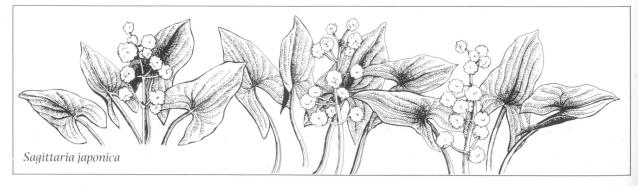

Sagittaria japonica

been noted in cultivation and this has paler green foliage and stiff erect sprays of blossoms, but it is *S. cernuus* that is most widely grown. Both can be increased easily by division of the clumps in early spring. 1 ft (30 cm).

Scirpus lacustris Bulrush. More correctly known now as *Schoenoplectus*, but still amongst gardeners as *Scirpus*, the bulrushes are a must for the garden pool. They are not the tall reeds commonly referred to as bulrushes with large brown poker-like heads, but slender green needle-like plants with tiny tassels of brownish flowers. It is *S. lacustris* which is the true bulrush – the one in which the infant Moses was said to have been cradled. This has slender green needle-like foliage which adds an architectural quality to the poolside. Propagation can be from seed, but division of the creeping rootstock in early spring is quite satisfactory. 2–3 ft (60–90 cm).

S. tabernaemontani Glaucous Bulrush. Usually growing 1 ft (30 cm) taller than *S. lacustris*, this can be rather too large for the average pool. Its greyish-green stems tend to dominate and the species itself is better replaced by the more modest growing 'Zebrinus' and 'Albescens'. This latter is usually attributed to *S. tabernaemontani*, but is believed to be of hybrid origin. This is of little account to the gardener as it displays magnificent needles of sulphurous white each with conspicuous longitudinal green stripes. The zebra rush, *S.t.* 'Zebrinus' is a fairly weak grower, but with handsome foliage that is alternately barred with green and white. Sometimes plain green shoots appear and these should be removed immediately. Propagation by division of the rootstock during early spring.

Sparganium ramosum Burr Reed. Although sometimes offered for the small pool, this handsome aquatic is rather rampant. It has rush-like leaves, brownish flowers and tiny teasel-like seed heads. Increased from seed or division. $1\frac{1}{2}$–3 ft (45–90 cm).

Typha angustifolia Narrow-leafed Reedmace. A tall handsome reedmace with slender grey-green leaves and striking brown poker-like seed heads. Generally too large for the garden pool. Propagation by division. 6 ft (1.8 m).

T. latifolia Reedmace. The most substantial reedmace with broad grey-green leaves and heavy chocolate-brown seed heads. Too large and invasive for most pools. Propagation by division in the spring. 6 ft (1.8 m).

T. minima A splendid miniature species with tiny brown poker-like heads amongst a waving sea of grassy foliage. Can be divided in the spring and is excellent for the small pool. $1\frac{1}{2}$ ft (45 cm).

T. stenophylla A modest version of the reedmace now often sold under its changed name, *T. laxmannii*. Typical foliage and seed heads. Increased readily by division. 3 ft (90 cm).

Veronica beccabunga Brooklime. A most useful scrambling native plant with more or less evergreen foliage and myriad tiny ultramarine flowers. Ideal for masking the edge of the pool. Easily increased from short stem cuttings taken during early spring and rooted in a pan of mud. 6–8 ins (15–20 cm).

Scirpus tabernaemontani 'Albescens'

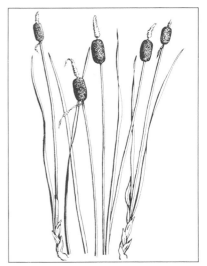

Typha minima

Veronica beccabunga

12. Floating Plants

Floating plants contribute to the balance of the pool by providing surface shade. This cuts down the amount of direct sunlight falling in the water and therefore makes life more difficult for the water-discolouring algae which attempt to dwell there. All are free-floating, gaining nourishment from the water and during the harsh winter months forming turions, or winter buds, which fall to the pool floor, remaining there until the summer sun warms the water once more. Most are purely functional, but some have decorative flowers and foliage as well. All are merely tossed on to the surface of the water, requiring no traditional form of planting.

Azolla caroliniana Fairy Moss. This is a tiny floating fern with lacy foliage which disappears entirely for the winter unless a portion is reduced and maintained in a jar or bowl of water in a frost-free place. A layer of soil should be distributed over the bottom of the jar or bowl and this will ensure that sufficient nutrients are available to sustain the plantlets until the spring. The benefits of maintaining fairy moss and similar floating subjects like this, are that early algal problems can be dealt with sooner. Algae invade water quickly when the sun starts to warm it up. This often turns the pool green initially because it takes the floating subjects much longer to start into growth and provide active competition.

Hydrocharis morsus-ranae Frogbit. Like a small floating waterlily, this little plant has delicate olive-green, kidney-shaped floating leaves and snow-white, three-petalled flowers. An excellent subject for the rock pool or sink garden, the frogbit also benefits from being partially maintained in a jar or bowl for the winter period.

Lemna minor Duckweed. A tiny-leafed floating plant familiar to most people as the green sward which smothers pools and streams in the countryside. Usually so prolific that the pool looks like a bright green carpet. Often sold

The invasive common duckweed (*Lemna minor***) almost covers the surface of this garden pond.**

for feeding goldfish, this is best avoided in the garden pool as it obscures the water from view, clings to all the marginal subjects, and is difficult to eliminate once established.

Lemna trisulca Ivy-leafed Duckweed. The least invasive of our native duckweeds. This is a non-carpeting kind, founding substantial underwater colonies which appear to float just beneath the surface of the water. The foliage is dark green, translucent, and of a crispy appearance.

Stratiotes aloides Water Soldier. A very distinctive floating aquatic which looks like the top of a pineapple. The leaves are long, slim and densely spiny along the edges, giving rise to charming pinkish or white papery blossoms during summer. As the season progresses young plantlets are produced on wiry runners in just the same way as young strawberry plants. The acidity or alkalinity of the water is said to have a bearing upon the level within the pool at which the plants float.

Trapa natans Water Chestnut. This handsome floating plant produces neat rosettes of rhomboidal leaves and unusual, papery white, axillary flowers throughout the summer. Technically an annual, the black horned nuts, which are freely produced, germinate readily and ensure a continuity of fresh plants. If the nuts are to be gathered in the autumn for storage until the following spring they must be kept moist in damp green sphagnum or a small jar of water. Dehydration kills the seeds.

Utricularia minor Lesser Bladderwort. A small fine-leafed, submerged floating plant with wands of tiny yellow, antirrhinum-like flowers above the surface of the water. The delicate filigree foliage is liberally sprinkled with tiny dark green bladders which capture unsuspecting insects and digest them.

U. vulgaris Greater Bladderwort. Similar to the lesser bladderwort, but with more showy, bright yellow flowers during July. This too has bladders amongst its foliage which lure and capture insects.

Wolffia arrhiza The tiniest of floating duckweeds, differing from the lemnas in that it remains rootless. The smallest flowering plant known to man and an interesting curiosity for the small pool or sink garden.

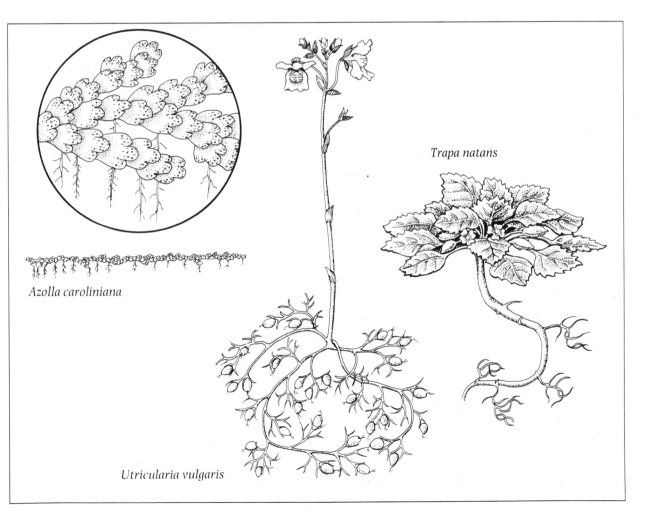

Trapa natans

Azolla caroliniana

Utricularia vulgaris

13. Submerged Oxygenating Plants

Submerged oxygenating plants occupy the lower reaches of the pool, and when they are first received from the nursery they may cause the new pool owner some consternation as they are invariably supplied as bunches of cuttings fastened together at the base with strips of lead. Although seeming to be clinging precariously to life, once introduced to the water, roots are rapidly initiated and the clump becomes quickly established.

Planting

Ideally, submerged plants should be planted in groups in proper aquatic planting baskets before being placed in the pool (see page 18). However, some pool owners think that this is troublesome and prefer to throw the bunches of plant into the water, allowing the weight of the lead to drag them base downwards to the bottom. This is quite satisfactory in an established pool where there is an accumulation of debris on the pool floor, or where a layer of soil has been introduced, as the plants then have something in which to anchor themselves. If the pool floor is bare and all the other plants are growing in containers the plants will exist, but more often than not the lead will rot through the stems of the cuttings and these will disintegrate and come floating to the surface of the water.

Choosing varieties

Selecting suitable oxygenating plants is only difficult because there are so many from which to choose. The majority will flourish in both alkaline or acid water if given an open sunny position. Some are more tolerant of moving water than others, while the gardener who has inherited a badly sited pool in the shade can even find a couple of sorts which will grow under those conditions. Almost all of them flower, but very few are worth including specifically on floral merit. Those that fulfil a dual role should receive priority.

Apium inundatum Water Celery. Very much like a small aquatic celery plant with pungent foliage and crowded heads of small white flowers above water level.

Callitriche hermaphroditica Autumnal Starwort. Luxuriant cress-like foliage which is beloved of goldfish. Stays completely submerged and persists throughout the winter (Illustrated on page 18.)

C. platycarpa Almost identical to the preceding, except that floating foliage is variously produced and the entire plant dies back for the winter months.

Ceratophyllum demersum Hornwort. Bristly, green, submerged plants which spend part of their life floating freely beneath the water, some of the time rooted to the pool floor and throughout the winter months as a tight resting bud. Will tolerate shade, deep and cool water.

Chara aspera Stonewort. Sometimes sold as a submerged oxygenating plant, the common stonewort is an intermediate between the higher plants and algae. It has coarse hairy foliage that has a pungent aroma.

Eleocharis acicularis Hair Grass. One of the few submerged plants that is not sold in a leaded bunch, but more usually as tiny clumps. It is a delicate little plant with bright green grassy leaves that spreads responsibly, clothing the entire surface of its container.

Elodea canadensis Canadian Pondweed. A well known but often despised submerged plant with a reputation for being invasive. While it is true that it can spread rather more quickly than many of its contemporaries, it is readily controlled and only likely to prove a nuisance in large areas of water. It has long arching stems with whorls of tiny green lance-shaped leaves.

Lobelia dortmanna

Fontinalis antipyretica Willow Moss. A handsome evergreen native with mossy dark green foliage. An excellent fish-spawning plant that is equally happy in moving water or still.

Hottonia palustris Water Violet. Although this is not the easiest submerged plant to get established, and really only a subject for the established pool, it is nevertheless the most beautiful of all the oxygenating plants.

Isoetes lacustris Quillwort. An amazing little fellow which is closely related to the ferns, but looks more like a submerged rush. This must have acid water if it is to produce its delicate dark green quills.

Lagarosiphon major Often referred to popularly as goldfish weed and botanically by its outdated name of *Elodea crispa*, this is the dark green curled plant that is sold in large quantities for goldfish bowls. It is a most useful plant as it grows freely and remains more or less evergreen.

Lobelia dortmanna Botanically a lobelia, this lovely little aquatic scarcely resembles the familiar blue lobelia of bedding schemes. It forms carpets of dense blunted foliage and produces tiny lavender-coloured blossoms on thin wiry stems.

Myriophyllum spicatum Spiked Milfoil. A delicate feathery plant with tiny crimson flowers. This is often planted by fish fanciers as a spawning plant for goldfish.

Myriophyllum verticillatum Whorled Milfoil. Long trailing stems with dense whorls of fine foliage and tiny greenish flowers. Another excellent spawning plant.

Oenanthe fluviatilis Water Dropwort. Dense carrot-like foliage both beneath and above the water crowned with myriad tiny white flowers during early summer. A submerged plant for shallower conditions in the larger pool.

Potamogeton crispus Curled Pondweed. The only one of this large group of submerged aquatics that can be unreservedly recommended. Handsome, crisped and crimped, underwater foliage of an attractive bronze-green colour. Tiny crimson spikes of flower are produced above the surface of the water during the summer, but these are of little consequence.

Ranunculus aquatilis Water Crowfoot. There are many crowfoots, but this is the loveliest. Handsome deeply dissected submerged foliage surmounted by white blossoms with bright yellow centres, themselves surrounded by floating green clover-like leaves. The best dual purpose submerged aquatic.

Tillaea recurva A very useful and hardy cress-like submerged plant with tiny white axillary flowers.

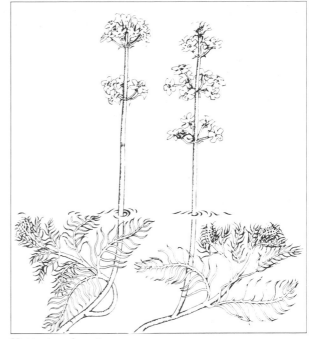

Hottonia palustris

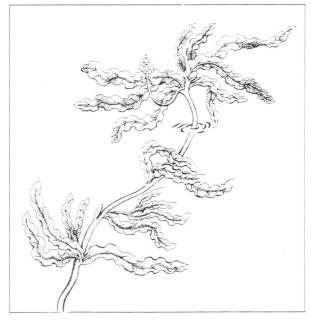

Potamogeton crispus

Ranunculus aquatilis

14. Bog Garden Plants

A bog garden is usually considered to be a natural extension of the garden pool, although this need not necessarily be so, for with modern lining materials like polythene and butyl rubber sheeting, damp areas in almost any part of the garden can be created with the minimum of fuss. Bog plants are naturally waterside subjects and one must concede that such a situation is really ideal, but that is not to say that they will not thrive in a moist bed that is artificially contrived in some other part of the garden.

A bog garden adjoining a pool is the simplest to make and maintain, particularly if catered for in the initial planning of the water garden. All that is required is a liner larger than necessary for the pool itself, the excess being spread out as a shallow pool about 12 ins (30 cm) deep. A retaining wall of loose bricks or stones must be laid to provide a barrier between the pool and the bog garden, the latter being filled with a peaty soil mixture over a layer of gravel.

This provides a moisture-retentive medium, but allows excess water to drain from the roots. Water from the pool moistens the soil through the barrier, the soil surface being at least 2 ins (5 cm) above the mean water level.

In other parts of the garden similar conditions can be provided by excavating an area of border and lining it with a polythene or butyl rubber sheet, the soil that is removed being well mixed with coarse peat before being replaced. This should be made wet and care taken during periods of warm weather to see that it does not dry out.

Choosing plants for a bog garden can be a formidable task, for nature does not clearly define what a bog plant is. To most gardeners though, bog plants can be said to be those that like moist conditions but not standing water. If treated as ordinary border plants they become stunted and the foliage scorched unless the season happens to be particularly wet.

All the following plants are good reliable bog plants which will tolerate a wide range of soil conditions. Acid-lovers are noted, all the others are lime-tolerant.

Aruncus sylvester Goat's Beard. A tall plant with creamy-white feathery plumes of flower and pale green, deeply cut leaves. A much shorter cultivar called 'Kneiffi' is of similar appearance but seldom grows taller than 3 ft (90 cm). Both flower throughout July and early August and can be increased by division during the winter.

Astilbe hybrids False Goat's Beard. Well known moisture-loving perennials with brightly coloured, feathery flower spikes. There are many very good cultivars available which flower for much of the summer. 'Peach Blossom' is salmon-pink, 'White Gloria' white and 'Red Sentinal' a good bright crimson. Heights vary, but most are around 3 ft (90 cm) except the tiny *crispa* cultivars like 'Lilliput' and 'Perkeo' which seldom exceed 6 ins (15 cm).

Cardamine pratensis Cuckoo Flower. A delightful spring-flowering subject with single rosy-lilac blossoms and delicate ferny foliage. There is a double form called *flore-plena* and this is even more lovely. Cuckoo flowers seldom grow more than 1 ft (30 cm) high and are easily increased by division in the autumn.

Filipendula ulmaria Meadow Sweet. Some would despise our native meadow sweet with its plumes of creamy-white frothy flowers, but few would dispute that the double form or its golden-leafed relative 'Aurea' have a right to a place in the modern bog garden. Both are increased by division during the winter. Flowers June–August.

Hosta fortunei One of the largest of the plantain lilies with handsome plain green leaves 1 ft (30 cm) or more long and bold spikes of lilac coloured funnel-shaped flowers in the summer.

Hosta glauca If anything an even larger leafed species with handsome glaucous heart-shaped leaves and spikes of whitish bell-shaped flowers.

Hosta lancifolia Not itself a particularly attractive species, but its golden-leafed progeny 'Aurea' and the green and white-leafed hybrid 'Thomas Hogg' are excellent foliage plants for the bog garden.

Hosta undulata medio-variegata A small plantain lily with twisted, undulating leaves of cream, white and green. All the hostas are readily increased by division during the spring.

Astilbe × arendsii

Iris kaempferi Japanese Clematis-Flowered Iris. Bold clumps of broad grassy leaves surmounted by the most exquisite velvety blooms imaginable. Many named varieties are available, but 'Blue Heaven', the deep violet 'Mandarin' and double rose-lavender 'Landscape at Dawn' are reliable. All must have an acid soil. Flowers mid-summer.

Iris sibirica Not as exotic looking as *I. kaempferi*, but much more tolerant of difficult soil conditions. All flower during June and early July with brightly coloured blossoms amongst clumps of grassy foliage. Many cultivars are available, but 'Perry's Blue', 'Snow Queen', and the deep violet-blue 'Emperor' are amongst the most popular. Both kinds of iris are best propagated by division immediately after flowering.

Lysichitum americanum Skunk Cabbage. A relative of the arums with huge yellow spathes during April, followed by large cabbagey leaves up to 3 ft (90 cm) tall.

Lysichitum camtschatcense A smaller plant from the Orient which produces creamy-white spathes during April. Both lysichitums are easily raised from seed if it is sown directly after harvesting on a tray of mud.

Lysimachia nummularia Creeping Jenny. A most useful evergreen carpeting plant for disguising the edge of a pond. Rarely growing more than 2 ins (5 cm) high it is lightened by sparkling yellow buttercup-like flowers for much of the summer. A cultivar called 'Aurea' has bright golden foliage.

Lysimachia punctata A strong-growing plant that has whorled spikes of bright yellow flowers in summer. Attaining a height of 2–3 ft (60–90 cm) it is a rather coarse plant, but most useful in difficult situations, especially on newly broken land.

Lythrum salicaria Purple Loosestrife. A very handsome native plant with candle-like spires of deep rose-pink flowers throughout the summer. Amongst the much improved cultivars are the bright pink 'Robert' and purple-flowered 'The Beacon'.

Iris kaempferi

This ample bog garden has room for generous quantities of primulas and iris. Foliage plants like the variegated hosta in the foreground prolong the display from early summer to later in the season.

Mimulus cardinalis Cardinal Monkey Flower. A hoary-leafed mimulus with bright scarlet-orange flowers which is not reliably hardy in cold winters. Although akin to those described under Marginal Plants it does not appreciate standing water. It grows about 1 ft (30 cm) high and is easily raised from seed or summer cuttings.

Parnassia palustris Grass of Parnassus. A rare and beautiful native which presents the gardener with a challenge. It has delicate little white flowers blotched with green and neat mounds of heart-shaped foliage. A lime-hater, it seldom grows more than 6 ins (15 cm) high and can be propagated from a spring sowing. Flowers July–September.

Peltiphyllum peltatum Umbrella Plant. An unusual plant with large bronze-green umbrella-like leaves some 3 ft (90 cm) high. In early spring before the leaves have appeared it produces neat globular heads of rose-coloured flowers on stout stems some $1\frac{1}{2}$ ft (45 cm) high.

Primula Many of the primulas, particularly the candelabra kinds, are bog garden subjects flourishing equally well in sun or shade where there is constant moisture. They all have distinctive rosettes of foliage from which arise wiry stems with tiered whorls of blooms or pendant bunches of brightly coloured blossoms. All are easily raised from seed, especially when this can be freshly obtained and sown immediately after collection.

Primula aurantiaca Bright orange blossoms in neat whorls during early May. $2\frac{1}{2}$ ft (75 cm).

Primula beesiana A candelabra species with rosy-purple flowers during June and July. 2 ft (60 cm).

Primula bulleyana

An orange-yellow candelabra type which flowers during June and July. $2\frac{1}{2}$ ft (75 cm).

Primula chungensis Seldom taller than 1 ft (30 cm), this little fellow delights everyone during June with a magnificent display of pale orange blossoms.

Primula denticulata Drumstick Primula. The earliest flowered primula with bold rounded heads of flowers during March and April. These are usually blue or lilac but in *alba* are pure white. They can be raised from root cuttings as well as seed and rarely grow more than 1 ft (30 cm) high.

Primula florindae Himalayan Cowslip. Attaining a height of 3 ft (90 cm) or more, this handsome, late summer-flowering primula is like an enormous cowslip with stout flower stems supporting pendant clusters of bright yellow flowers.

Primula helodoxa A vigorous kind up to 3 ft (90 cm) tall when in conditions to its liking. It is somewhat later than most other bog garden primulas; golden flowers in mid-July or early August.

Primula japonica One of the most popular candelabra kinds with bright crimson blooms in summer and fresh green leaves. 'Miller's Crimson' is a superior red cultivar and 'Postford White' the best white form.

Primula microdonta alpicola A charming little plant with drooping soft yellow blooms on stems no more than a 1 ft (30 cm) high. These have earned it the popular name of moonlight primula. There is a deep violet-mauve flowered form called *violacea* as well.

Primula pulverulenta One of the best candelabra kinds, for not only has it

Peltiphyllum peltatum

Primula japonica 'Postford White'

Hosta fortunei

Iris sibirica

Lysichitum camtschatcense

attractive magenta blossoms but distinctive white mealy stems as well. 'Bartley Strain' is equally beautiful, sporting flowers that range through buff to pink and with the same distinctive mealiness. Rarely growing taller than 2 ft (60 cm), they provide a sparkling show during May and early June.

Primula rosea Flowering during March and April, this little gem has vivid rose-pink blossoms on stems a few inches high. The improved cultivar 'Delight', unlike the species, must be increased by division rather than seed.

Primula sikkimensis Closely allied to *P. florindae*, this is a much shorter cowslip-like plant no more than 1 ft (30 cm) high. It flowers around the same time with bright yellow flowers and handsome green leaves which have a purplish caste.

Primula vialii Looking rather like a dwarf red-hot-poker than a primula, this little beauty should find its way into every bog garden. Unlike all the previous species, this produces its blossoms in congested clusters on short stout spikes. The unopened buds at the top of the spike are red while the lower open flowers are lilac. Sadly this is not a long-lived species and must be regularly replaced from seed.

Rheum palmatum Ornamental Rhubarb. There are a number of ornamental rhubarbs about, but this is the most reliable. Reaching a height of 6 ft (1.8 m) when flowering, it is the striking foliage which makes it so worthwhile, particularly where there is a little shade. 'Bowles Crimson' is an improved cultivar with a strong red infusion in the leaves.

Rodgersia aesculifolia Enjoying damp rather than wet conditions, this lovely little fellow has foliage like that of a horse chestnut. During summer frothy heads of creamy-white blossoms are produced on stems 3 ft (90 cm) high.

Rodgersia tabularis Pale green circular plate-like leaves are the hall mark of this very popular plant. It flowers too, but not until midsummer when it thrusts up dense panicles of creamy-white blossoms.

Trollius europaeus Globe Flower. Spring-flowering perennials with attractive large globular buttercup-like heads in yellow or orange. There are innumerable cultivars of which the intense orange 'Fire Globe', soft yellow 'Canary Bird' and beautifully formed 'Orange Princess' are amongst the best. They can be easily divided during early spring, just as they are breaking into growth.

Bog garden ferns

Matteucia struthiopteris Ostrich Feather Fern. A bright green shuttle-cock fern which enjoys moist poolside conditions. It increases by rhizomes which push up young shuttlecocks at random.

Onoclea sensibilis Sensitive Fern. A creeping fern with erect flattened fronds up to 2 ft (60 cm) high. In spring these are an attractive pink colour, but turn to lime-green with age.

Osmunda regalis Royal Fern. One of the tallest and most handsome hardy ferns. Pale green foliage which ages to bronze. There are crested, undulate and purple foliage kinds too. 4–6 ft (1.2 m–1.8 m).

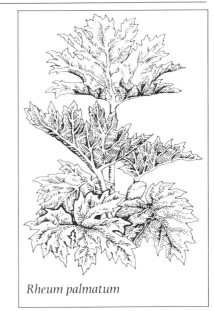

Rheum palmatum

Rodgersia tabularis

Trollius europaeus

Matteucia struthiopteris

Osmunda regalis

15. Some Good Half-hardy Aquatics

It may seem folly to attempt to grow tender aquatics in our fickle climate, but some are such rapid growers and so decorative that they can quite easily be treated as temporary inhabitants of the garden pool, or else grown in tubs or sinks. Indeed, the tropical waterlilies seem to respond better to tub culture than any other method.

Tropical waterlilies

These are probably the most important tender aquatics for temporary cultivation in a temperate climate. Some quite clearly will be seen to require tropical temperatures before giving of their best, while others are almost hardy in the milder parts of the country. The great joy with tropical waterlilies is that they almost all become dormant during the winter months and can be stored conveniently in damp sand. They are also available in colours which are noticeably absent from their hardy cousins.

In early spring, when tropical waterlilies become available from the nurserymen they are usually still in their dormant state and appear as rather coarse rounded chestnut-like tubers. These require sprouting in a fairly warm temperature in pots of a soil-based compost in a bucket of water with the crown situated just below water level. Depending upon the temperature and light intensity, but after a couple of weeks, vigorous young shoots should appear. At this stage the waterlilies should be lifted and planted in proper aquatic planting baskets prior to being placed out in the pool, or else planted individually in tubs, barrels or similar containers. It is important that tropical waterlilies are not put outside until all danger of frost has passed. Summer maintenance is the same as for their hardy counterparts.

As the leaves start to die back during the autumn, the tubers should be lifted and gradually dried off until all fleshy foliage has perished. This must not be a sudden experience for the plant. The tuber should be kept reasonably damp, but not wet, at all times. Damp sand is the best medium to use for storage, particularly if used in conjunction with an airtight biscuit or cake tin. In any case precautions should be taken to protect the tubers from vermin, which find them a great delicacy. When selecting tubers for storage always choose the younger vigorous ones. Old woody tubers are more difficult to keep through the winter and are often reluctant to sprout the following spring.

There are myriad tropical waterlily cultivars to choose from, but several are well known as reliable for a cooler climate. There are both night-blooming and day-flowering kinds.

DAY-BLOOMING HYBRIDS
Nymphaea 'Blue Beauty' An old reliable variety with deep blue flowers with a central golden disc. Prefers between $2\frac{1}{2}$–3 ft (75–90 cm) of water.
N. 'General Pershing' Huge pink blossoms held well above the water on stout stems. The young buds have conspicuous purple stripes; the leaves are green streaked with red. $2\frac{1}{2}$–3 ft (75–90 cm) of water.
N. 'Mrs. George H. Pring' Large, white, starry blossoms and fresh green leaves smeared reddish-brown. From 1 ft (30 cm) of water to 3 ft (90 cm).

NIGHT-BLOOMING HYBRIDS
N. 'B. C. Berry' Immense shallow blossoms of amaranth-purple. Medium-sized leaves with a purplish mottling and heavily indented margins. Needs between $1\frac{1}{2}$–$2\frac{1}{2}$ ft (45–75 cm) of water.
N. 'Emily Grant Hutchings' Cup-shaped blossoms of pinkish-red with deep amaranth stamens. Both sepals and foliage have a bronzed-crimson overlay. Prefers between $1\frac{1}{2}$–$2\frac{1}{2}$ ft (45–75 cm) of water.
N. 'Missouri' Large pure white flowers on stout stems held high above the water. Dark green leaves with purple and brown mottling and conspicuously indented margins. At least $2\frac{1}{2}$ ft (75 cm) of water.

The species of tropical waterlily can be increased by seed, but the named kinds can only be propagated by division, young tubers or, on certain occasions, by plantlets borne on the leaves.

Nelumbo nucifera (Sacred Lotus)

Other half-hardy aquatics

Eichhornia crassipes Water Hyacinth. A most attractive floating plant that will grace the pool for much of the summer. Its clusters of shiny green leaves with grossly inflated bases produced magnificent blue and lilac orchid-like flowers. It can be floated on the pool during early June when all danger of frost has passed, young plants being returned to a bucket of water in a frost-free greenhouse for the winter months. Propagation is by separating out the young plantlets and allowing them to follow an independent life. Height 6–8 ins (15–20 cm).

Nelumbo nucifera Sacred Lotus. The famous lotus of the East. A tall growing plant with waxy plate-like leaves held on stout leaf stems. Immense blossoms up to 1 ft (30 cm) across which open a vivid rose colour but age to soft flesh-pink.

This spectacular tropical aquatic responds well to the tub culture. Its strange banana-like rootstocks come to hand during early spring and are planted horizontally in the same medium as recommended for waterlilies in tubs, to which sufficient water is added to cover the soil. As the rootstocks sprout, the water level is gradually raised. Occasionally support will be needed for the immense foliage, but in sheltered situations it usually takes care of itself. The attractive large blossoms are followed by interesting seed pods, like tiny watering-can roses. These can be dried and used in dry floral arrangements. The root-stocks are lifted and stored in sand, like the tubers of tropical waterlilies, for the winter months.

There are many cultivars of nelumbo available from specialists, but the North American species *N. pentapetala* is more likely to be encountered. This is shorter growing than *N. nucifera*, rarely attaining a height of more than 3 ft (90 cm) and with flowers of pale sulphur-yellow. Propagation of all kinds is by separation of the rootstock, although the species are easily raised from seed.

Thalia dealbata This half-hardy aquatic is splendid for decorating the outdoor pool during summer. It has bold greyish-green leaves up to 5 ft (1.5 m) high and sprays of purplish blossoms during summer. It looks very much like an aquatic version of the canna, a popular bedding subject.

Eichhornia crassipes (Water Hyacinth)

16. Raising Your Own Plants

Waterlilies

Most waterlilies can be readily propagated from 'eyes'. These are small growing points which appear along the rootstocks of mature healthy plants. For the most part they appear as tiny versions of the main growing point, each with its juvenile foliage ready to burst into active growth, although some kinds have brittle rounded nodules which can be easily detached.

Established plants can be carefully lifted during early summer and the 'eyes' removed with a sharp knife. The wounds of both eye and rootstock should then be dusted with sulphur or charcoal in order to prevent infection and the parent plant returned to the pool. The severed eyes can then be potted individually in small pots in a good clean garden soil and stood in a shallow container of water with just the growing points submerged. If the eyes are very small it would be wise to keep them in a frame, greenhouse or on the kitchen windowsill.

When the leaf stalks of the young waterlilies lengthen, the water level can be raised. As they develop further they will require potting into progressively larger pots. When large enough to support themselves in the rough and tumble of the garden pool, they can be potted in a proper waterlily planting basket and placed in the pool in their permanent positions.

Waterlilies from seed

Some of the miniature waterlilies do not produce eyes and therefore must be increased from seed. This must be freshly collected from ripened seed pods and not have been allowed to dry out. When harvested properly, the seed will be enclosed in a gelatinous substance and this should be sown with the seed. Attempts at teasing the individual seed out with a pair of tweezers are unnecessary and time-consuming.

The best sowing medium is a good, clean, heavy loam with stones or any similar objects sieved out. Shallow pans are filled with this and the jelly-like mass containing the seeds spread as evenly as possible over the surface. A light covering of soil should be given and the pans watered liberally from a watering-can with a fine rose attachment. This will settle the compost nicely and drive troublesome air out of the compost. The pans can then be stood in a bowl or aquarium with the water just over the surface of the compost.

Within a week or two the first seedlings will appear. These have tiny transluscent lanceolate leaves and look rather like liverworts. It is at this time and for the next few months that filamentous algae makes itself a nuisance, becoming entangled amongst the fragile juvenile foliage of the seedlings. One of the proprietary pool algaecides correctly administered should help control the problem.

When the floating leaves start coming to the surface of the water the plants will be ready for pricking out. They should be lifted in clumps and washed thoroughly to remove all the soil and then gently teased apart. A plastic seed tray is the most useful container in which to prick out waterlily seedlings, submerging it so that the compost is about 1 in (2.5 cm) beneath the surface of the water. The water level is then adjusted as growths lengthen and become stronger. After six months or so the compost will have become exhausted and the seedlings crowded. At this time they can be carefully lifted and removed to their permanent homes.

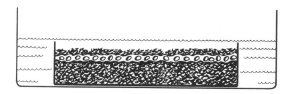

Sowing waterlily seed

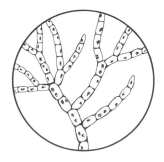

Algae magnified × 250

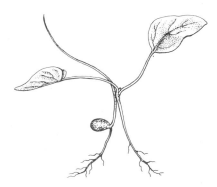

Waterlily seedling

Reeds and rushes

Reeds and rushes like typha and scirpus are propagated by division which should be undertaken in the spring. Large clumps that need dividing are handled in the same way as herbaceous perennials, but the temptation to cut the foliage right back should be resisted. A number of reeds and rushes have hollow stems and if these are cut so severely that water can enter, they rot away.

Creeping aquatics

Creeping aquatics like the bog bean, *Menyanthes trifoliata*, and bog arum, *Calla palustris*, must have wet conditions to make satisfactory growth. The division of their scrambling rhizomes is the easiest method of reproduction. Menyanthes is merely chopped into small sections of stem, each with a latent bud and preferably a vestige of root attached, and then planted in trays of mud until established and sprouting. Calla can be handled in the same way, but dormant buds that arise along the rhizome can be detached readily and planted out independent of the old stem. The same can be done with the flowering rush *Butomus umbellatus*, for tiny bulbils appear in the axils of the leaves where they arise from the hard woody rhizome. If planted in trays of mud they rapidly turn into healthy young plants.

Some creeping aquatics are better increased from cuttings taken in the spring when the shoots are about 2 ins (5 cm) long. These include the water mint, *Mentha aquatica* and the common brooklime, *Veronica beccabunga*. Water forget-me-not, *Myosotis scorpioides*, can be increased from cuttings with a little root attached or by division, while some people raise the improved cultivar 'Semperflorens' from seed.

A cutting of an aquatic is taken and rooted in wet soil.

Aquatics from seed

Seed raising is an obvious method of propagation for many aquatic plants, including those like the bog arum which have just been discussed. However, it is a slower process and plants may take up to three months longer to attain plantable size. Seed raising of aquatics is still something of a hit and miss affair, for little research has been done on the subject and no two species seem to require identical conditions. The pickerel, *Pontederia cordata*, must be sown while still green, whereas the water plantain, *Alisma plantago-aquatica*, will grow if the seed is twelve months old.

The water hawthorn, *Aponogeton distachyus*, will grow either if sown immediately it ripens or if kept until the following year, but it loses its viability if allowed to dry out completely.

Most decorative aquatic plants, when raised from seed, prosper in a soil-based seed compost. Never use a potting compost as this will have fertiliser in it in sufficient quantities to cause rapid algal growth in the water. Seedlings should be pricked out as soon as they are large enough to handle, most benefiting from being grown in small pots rather than seed trays.

17. Choosing Fish for the Pool

While those pool owners who regard themselves first and foremost as gardeners may not be too concerned whether they introduce fish to the pool, there are sound reasons for doing so. In practical terms, the presence of fish will control undesirable mosquito larvae, which if left to their own devices will soon make life uncomfortable for the gardener, certainly in the immediate vicinity of the pool. As well as devouring mosquito larvae, decorative pond fish are also fond of other aquatic insect pests such as caddis flies and waterlily aphids. On the ornamental side, it must be agreed that a pool without fish is a lifeless place. The addition of a few brightly coloured goldfish brings the underwater picture to life.

It is unwise to introduce ornamental fish to a pool until at least two or three weeks after planting. Aquatic plants need time to establish themselves before fish start brushing against them and poking about in the planting baskets. It is unnecessary to introduce large fish to the pool at the outset, as quite small fish will rapidly assume adult proportions if given plenty of space. It is unwise to introduce more than 2 ins (5 cm) length of fish per square foot of the surface area of the deeper part. A maximum of 6 ins (15 cm) length of fish can be achieved eventually, but beyond this casualties will occur as the pool then becomes unbalanced. The calculation of length of fish is based upon the collective length of all the pool inmates and includes the tail (see page 19).

Selecting the fish

While not decrying the efforts of mail order suppliers of cold-water fish, it is far more satisfactory to visit a retailer locally and choose your own, even if it is only from the relatively limited selection in the corner pet shop. Good health and conformation are much more likely to result from personal selection, and in the case of goldfish and shubunkins, specific colours can be chosen.

The majority of pondfish sold in this country are imported. The common goldfish and shubunkins come from Italy, golden orfe from Germany and fancy goldfish and both Higoi and Nishiki Koi carp from Singapore or Japan. Some people are concerned by the fact that many of our commercial fish stocks are derived from much warmer climates, but there need be no concern, for the fact that they have come from warmer water does not affect their hardiness and often means that their colouration is more intense than if they were raised in cooler waters. It is the long journey that should give rise to doubts, for many retailers start selling fish before they are properly rested and the travel-weary ones succumb. Very bright colour usually indicates recent arrival. It is always better to go for a faded fish, for this is likely to have been in the retailer's tank longer. Once introduced to the rich mellow waters of a garden pool, paler fish become dark and handsome once more.

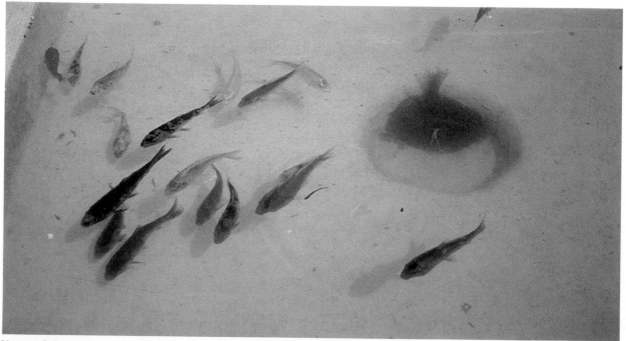

Young fish which are ready for sale are displayed in a retailer's tank.

Signs of health

The most important consideration when buying pond fish is health. This applies especially when purchasing fish to add to an existing collection. One dubious character introduced to a pool of strong healthy fish will cause problems very quickly. In any event, it is desirable to isolate new acquisitions for a couple of weeks to make sure that they are quite healthy, although in the case of white spot disease (see page 61) this is often not long enough.

All coldwater fish, irrespective of form or species, have stiff erect fins if they are in good health. Lively fish are often not especially healthy fish, but hungry fish. It is a common dealer's ploy to keep fish a little hungry to ensure that they do not become lethargic and also ensure that they do not foul the water unduly during travelling. Foul water can lead to losses through suffocation, and is a valid reason for not being too generous with the goldfish food. All fish with scales missing should be regarded with suspicion, especially the smaller sizes, which often become quickly infected with fungus. Larger specimens can more readily cope with this secondary infection which is easily and economically treated on larger fish. Indeed, some fish seem to pick up patches of fungus during the winter, but this is of minor importance. As a routine precaution it is useful to dip every newly acquired fish in a proprietary fungus cure. Those based upon methylene blue or malachite green are quick and effective.

Getting the fish home

The majority of retailers pack their fish in large heavy-gauge polythene bags with a little water, the void being blown up with oxygen. This is the most satisfactory means of packaging and can be recommended for any fish except orfe on hot or sultry days. Orfe have a high oxygen requirement and are best moved during cool or rainy weather.

When introducing fish to the pool, float the bag on the surface of the water until the water temperature in the bag falls to roughly the same as that of the pool. However, if the day is very hot it is better to take a chance and tip the fish into the pool immediately; imprisoned in the bag on a warm day they may expire before the water temperature is equalised. A sudden change of water temperature can have an effect upon the swim bladder and the creature's sense of balance, causing them to swim in a violent corkscrew-like fashion or upside-down just beneath the surface of the water.

All fish that have been freshly introduced to a pool will benefit from feeding, but it may be several days before they show themselves regularly. To begin with, they will doubtless hide amongst submerged plants and the floating leaves of waterlilies, but after a week or so will settle down and be observed basking in the sunshine.

These shubunkins will rise boldly to the surface to be fed.

18. Breeding a Few Fish

Most pool owners like to try breeding a few fish, even if they eventually have to give them away to friends. However, for some, fish breeding has its serious side and in many cases the garden pool is not planted so much for the benefit of the human eye as for the well-being and proliferation of the fish.

All the fish that the pool owner is likely to have will belong to the carp family. Therefore they all have similar requirements for their successful reproduction, although certain species, notably orfe and tench, seem loath to breed freely in captivity in this country.

Selecting breeding fish

Many people start breeding fish by purchasing one or two matched pairs of goldfish. While this is to be recommended, it does not follow that the pair purchased will breed with each other if there are other sexually mature fish in the pond. Generally like breed with like, but hybrids in the carp family are common and those of similar shape and constitution do interbreed.

All the species known collectively as carp, and of course the common goldfish and its forms, reproduce freely and many interbreed with one another.

The breeding season lasts from late spring until late summer, the sexual urges of the fish being stimulated by the warmth and light intensity associated with these seasons. Most goldfish are sexually mature in their second year, although adulthood is related more directly to size than age. Any goldfish 3 ins (8 cm) or more in length should be capable of reproduction.

Sexing fish in the spring is fairly easy. Body shape when looked at from above is oval or elliptical for the female fish and slim and pencil-like for the male, the male being further enhanced by the appearance of white pimples or nuptial tubercles which are sprinkled liberally over his gill plates and often on top of his head as well.

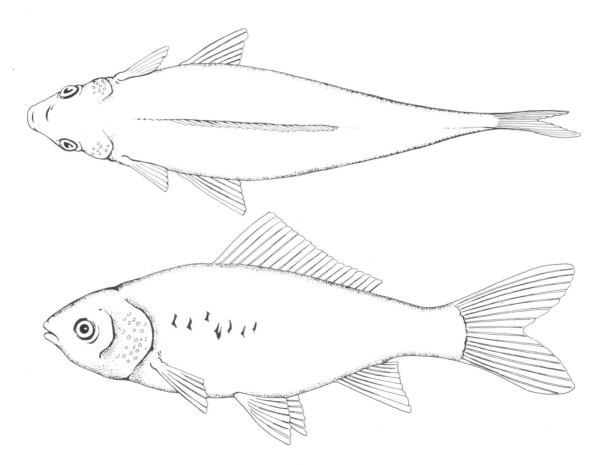

Male fish – notice the tubercles on the gills and the body shape from above.

Spawning

Spawnings occur at any time during the breeding season, several taking place each year. Their frequency is unpredictable and seems to be linked to water temperature rather than any other definable factor. During spawning the male fish chases the female around the pool and amongst the submerged plants, brushing and pushing furiously against her flanks. The female then releases the spawn, trailing it in and amongst the stems and foliage of submerged plants. The male releases his milt or sperm-bearing fluid amongst the eggs which then become fertilised. When this has happened the adults should, if possible, be separated from the area in which the spawn has been deposited. Alternatively plants covered in spawn can be removed to an aquarium containing pond water. The use of the same water is most important, as it will be of the same temperature and chemical composition as that in the pool and consequently not injurious to the sensitive eggs.

Within three or four days the fry will be seen to be developing. Initially they are difficult to see, resembling tiny pins in the water clinging to submerged plants. After a couple of weeks they are recognisable as fish, sometimes transparent, occasionally bronze, but all eventually attaining their correct adult propor-

tions. Often fish will remain bronze until quite large, sometimes not changing to the rich oranges, reds and yellows normally associated with goldfish. This delay in colour change is caused by the water temperature. The lower the water temperature at spawning, the longer that it will take for the youngsters to change colour.

Baby fish require feeding, especially if they are confined initially to a bucket with just a few plants lying in it. For the first few days they have their own food reserve, but towards the end of the first week will be feeling rather hungry. Special baby fish foods are available from water garden centres and pet stores. These come in tubes rather like toothpaste and are simply squeezed into the water every couple of days. If these are not available locally, a little chopped boiled egg will serve as well. In a large pool fry are generally well able to take care of themselves as regards feeding. Putting in baby fish food is wasteful as the adults will simply devour the lot.

Irrespective of the pool owner's attention, if there are goldfish and carp in the pool and the sexes are reasonably evenly balanced, breeding will take place and a handful of young fish will almost certainly be raised successfully.

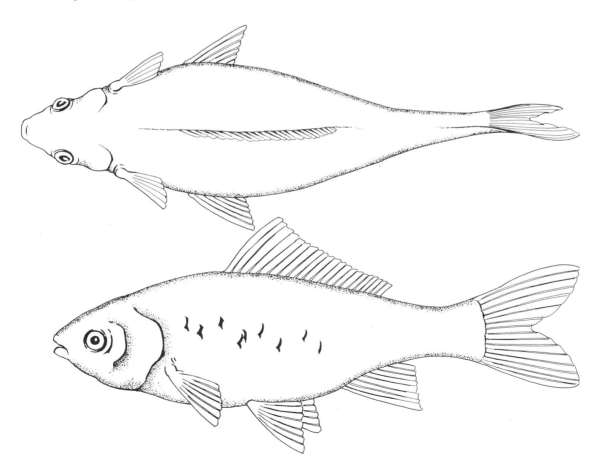

Female fish

19. Ornamental Pond Fish

All the decorative pool fish described here will co-exist happily. It is only fry that are vulnerable. All coldwater fish grow in accordance with their surroundings. A tiny goldfish which has been confined to a bowl for a number of years will start to grow lustily once introduced to the spaciousness of a garden pool. It is therefore impossible to judge the age of a fish by its size, but any fish 3 ins (8 cm) in length or more will be mature enough to be capable of breeding.

Goldfish

This is the most popular of all coldwater fish and is available in a range of colours that extends from the common red and orange, through pink and yellow to white. It is a hardy and robust fish which will survive even severe winters outdoors provided that there is a depth of at least 1½ ft (45 cm) of water in one part of the pool.

Apart from differences in colour, the most striking variation within the goldfish family is the transparent scaled form – the shubunkin. In this the body appears to be smooth and scaleless, revealing all kinds of colour combinations and embracing shades of blue and violet which do not occur in the common goldfish. In addition to the wide range of mixed colours available, there are named strains, much in the same way as we have named varieties of garden flowers. These occur most commonly in the shubunkins, Bristol Blue and Cambridge Blue being the two most desirable strains for the enthusiastic fish keeper. The former has a base colour of blue, heavily overlaid with violet and mauve and liberally splashed with crimson. The Cambridge Blue is of a soft powder-blue shade with a violet overlay and patches of ochre.

Goldfish – fancy varieties

Most of the fancy goldfish are the prerogative of the keen fish keeper rather than the average water gardener. While being extremely attractive, they are also notoriously temperamental, and require the kind of attention which most pool owners are unlikely to be prepared to give. Unless great care is taken to ensure their survival in the winter they will become no more than transitory inhabitants of the pool.

The exceptions are the comet-longtailed varieties of both goldfish and shubunkins. These appear as conventional fish, but with greatly extended tails that may be equal in length to the body. They are extremely graceful and hardy, and add an exotic touch to the garden pool. So too would the fantails and moors if they were a little more robust. Often sold as ornamental pond fish, and sometimes living happily as such, they are more properly accommodated in a coldwater aquarium.

Fantails are dumpy round-bodied goldfish with spreading tripartite tails. They are usually available in red, orange and white, or very often a combination of those colours. The moors are of similar appearance, but velvety black and with protruding eyes. Red, and red and white forms of the latter are generally referred

to as telescopes on account of their telescopic eyes.

Veil-tails are the same as fantails, but with longer tail fins which hang very much like a veil. The oranda is a further departure from the veil-tail and has curious strawberry-like growths on its head, while the lion-head has no dorsal fin and an exaggerated excrescence which decorates the head like a lion's mane. Bubble-eyes have protruding bubble-like eyes and celestials are somewhat flattened about the head with curious upward-pointing eyes. These fancy kinds are frequently offered to pond owners, but their purchase should be tempered with caution.

Unfortunately fancy goldfish varieties are promiscuous and fry from a fancy female will yield a progeny of unknown specification unless a deliberate union has been made between two breeding fish of the same class.

Bronze carp

These cheap and cheerful fish are often offered by retailers for the garden pool. Their parentage cannot always be determined, but more often than not they are uncoloured goldfish. When goldfish spawn, the water temperature at that time has a direct bearing upon the time it will take the majority of the progeny to attain the correct hue. Most juvenile fish are an attractive chocolate-bronze colour, but progressively take on their adult livery as the season passes. Some, which are the result of spawn deposited at a low temperature, take several years to change, while others remain bronze indefinitely. These are of little monetary value to the fish breeder and are sold as bronze carp. They are useful in so far as they may change to bright colours after a spell in the pool, otherwise they are barely discernible in the murky depths. When stocking a large area of water their use can be more readily justified.

Common carp

It is best to regard the common carp and other related species such as mirror carp, crucian carp and leather carp as fish for the larger pool. While the crucian carp is very closely allied to the goldfish it is not so well behaved and, being a dull colour, does not greatly enhance the watery scene. The others are equally uninteresting in the small pool, grubbing around amongst the plants and generally making themselves a bit of a nuisance. In the large pool their inclusion will add interest and variety without causing any problem.

The small pool owner must look to both Higoi and Nishiki Koi carp to provide the necessary variety. Both strains are exceedingly beautiful and a specimen or two of each can be recommended for all but the tiniest of pools. The Higoi carp is often referred to as the Chinese red carp, although its body colouration is more of a salmon-pink than a red. It is a chubby, meaty fish with a broad deep body, somewhat depressed head and a pair of distinctive pendant barbels. The Nishiki Koi or Koi carp is of similar stature, often without the barbels, but with a strong blunt head and deep chunky body. These are available in the widest colour range imaginable, some having glossy metallic scales in vivid orange and yellow hues, while others look rather like refined shubunkins. There are named varieties available too, with Japanese names like Ki-ogen, Sanke and Bekko, but one needs to be well endowed financially in order to obtain quality fish of these carefully bred strains.

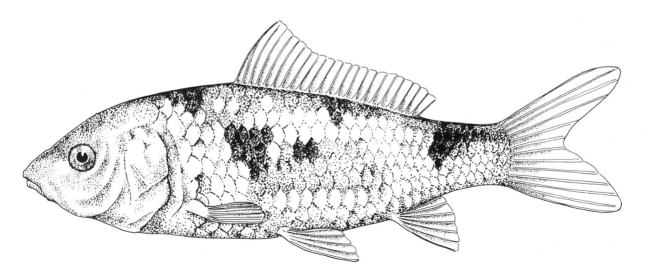

Koi carp

Orfe

While most ornamental fish inhabit the middle regions of the pool, the orfe spend most of their lives just beneath the surface. The common kind is the silver orfe, whose silvery body has the appearance of a refined sardine. An interesting fish, it does not enjoy the popularity of its golden variety. Not strictly a gold colour, more a salmon-pink or orange, the golden orfe adds colour and life to the pool. It is a slender pencil-like fish, which is happiest when swimming about in shoals, so it is preferable to purchase at least four initially. But do not be tempted by large individuals, for these have a high oxygen requirement and are extremely difficult to get home from the retailer without losses. A cold wet day provides the best chance of success. Sunshine or thundery weather are certain trouble when transporting orfe. To overcome this problem purchase smaller sizes. A 2 ins (5 cm) fish may attain a length of 6 ins (15 cm) in a single season. Apart from adding sparkle to the pool, orfe delight old and young alike with their antics, whether it be leaping for flies on a still evening or dancing in the cascading water of a fountain.

Rudd

These are similar in shape and appearance to the orfe, but will more readily inhabit greater areas of the pool. The common rudd is a silvery colour with bright red fins and a healthy appetite for filamentous algae, while its more desirable golden form is of similar appearance with a bronzed or coppery cast. They rarely breed in the small pool, but in larger expanses of water, where there is abundant underwater plant life, they reproduce freely.

Roach

Essentially a river fish, the roach is sometimes offered by water gardening specialists. It adapts well to pond life, but would not relish being confined to a small pool. It has a most distinguished steel-grey body and haunting red irises to its eyes, and is often confused with the dace which, although of similar appearance, does not have the characteristic red eyes of the roach. The dace is a fish of expansive waters and should be considered very carefully before being introduced to the garden pool.

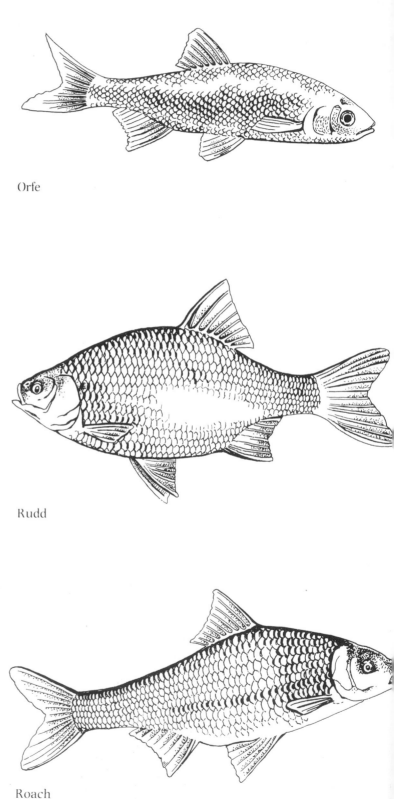

Orfe

Rudd

Roach

Bitterling

Many people regard this as a fish for the coldwater aquarium, but it is completely hardy, and although not long-lived, is a valuable addition to the pond community. Looking rather like a small carp, but with a lustrous metallic sheen, it is a lively little fellow that compensates for its lack of size with an extraordinary and bizarre life cycle which can be carefully observed in a small pool.

Breeding bitterling take on vivid colours, especially the males which turn an intense blue or mauve. The females are a more subdued hue, but prior to spawning produce long ovipositors or egg-laying tubes which are used to deposit the eggs in the mantle cavity of a living freshwater mussel, usually the Painter's Mussel (see page 51). Eggs are laid two or three at a time, after which the male fish ejects his milt or sperm-bearing fluid into the inhalant siphon of the mussel thus bringing about fertilisation. Incubation takes place within the mussel and continues for about three weeks. The fry remain with their host for some time after hatching, leaving only when they are capable of leading an independent existence.

Other aquatic creatures

Apart from ornamental fish, other aquatic creatures make their home in the garden pool uninvited. These sometimes cause the pool owner some alarm, although most are harmless and add considerable interest to the feature.

FROGS These splendid creatures are marvellous additions to pond life, feeding on harmful insect pests, producing tadpoles and splashing around in an eccentric manner. Beloved of small boys, these lumbering amphibians rarely cause any problem. The bad reputation which they have in some quarters has been derived from occasional reports of male frogs clasping adult fish in a mating embrace and causing damage to the unfortunate host. These occurrences are rare and only occur in pools where there are no female frogs.

TOADS Great friends of the gardener because of their preferred diet of slugs and other garden pests, toads are not so frequently seen in the pool, although their spawn is often deposited there. Every encouragement should be given to retain these characters and a stone or two placed in the vicinity, beneath which they can hide, is a good investment.

NEWTS Confused with lizards by many folk, these insectivorous amphibians are common visitors to the garden pool. The common newt is a brownish or olive colour, the male being enhanced by a rippling crest along its back and a reddish or orange belly. Common newts only live in the water for a short period of time, carrying out their courtship and depositing eggs in the water. For the remainder of the year they rest beneath stones during the heat of the day and become torpid and more or less hibernate during the winter.

Great crested newts, on the other hand, live for most of the year in the water, where they breed successfully. Lovely black lizard-like amphibians with brilliant yellow bellies, their very survival depends upon us giving them sanctuary in garden pools. In the wild they are extremely scarce and are now legally protected.

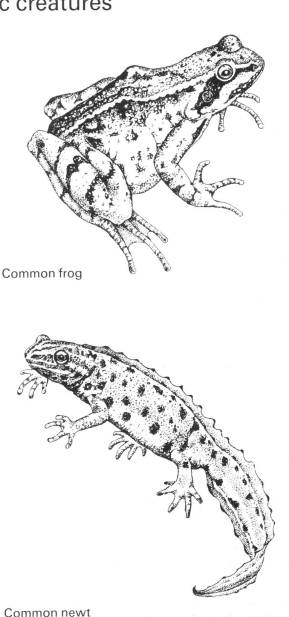

Common frog

Common newt

20. The Pool in Spring and Summer

Spring is the time for planting new aquatic plants and introducing fish to an established pool. It is the time to lift and divide overcrowded waterlilies and marginal plants and generally reassess the situation in the light of winter losses. It is always difficult to know whether all the floating plants have survived until the water is warmed by the spring sunshine and they reappear at the surface. All the other subjects should certainly be showing signs of active growth by late April, so empty containers can be removed and replanted with fresh stock.

Applying fertiliser

When plants are lifted, divided and repotted they are placed in a revitalised soil which will require little additional feeding for a couple of years. Longer established plants need a certain amount of nourishment and this has to be carefully administered to prevent the entire pool going green. Fertilisers provide mineral salts for the ever-present algae which reproduce rapidly and create an unpleasant green bloom. It is therefore vital that any fertiliser that is given is naturally a slow-release type and is as close to the recipient plant as possible. It is possible now to purchase little sachets of aquatic plant fertiliser with tiny pin-prick holes which allow the absorption of the fertiliser. These sachets are intended to be placed next to each plant and pushed down into the growing medium. Equally effective fertilisation can be carried out with coarse bonemeal mixed with heavy soil or clay in the form of bonemeal 'pills'. Take a good handful of coarse bonemeal and mix it with clay or heavy soil so that a 'pill' is formed about as large as a billiard ball. This can then be pushed into the compost in the planting basket next to the plant. As plant foods are released slowly the plant for which they are intended is most likely to benefit. More liberal use of the fertiliser soon creates algal problems by escaping freely into the water.

A sachet of fertiliser is pushed into the soil.

Feeding fish

While few gardeners consider feeding their aquatic plants on a regular basis, most delight in feeding the decorative fish in their pond. In the initial establishment of a pool it is useful to feed fish, but once a balance has been created there is no necessity to continue feeding. A well balanced pool that is not over-populated with fish will have sufficient aquatic life to sustain the health and vigour of the inhabitants. However, most pool owners like to feed their fish on a regular basis and there is no reason why they should not. Goldfish will not actively seek prey if they are provided with regular meals and after a short period of time will react immediately to a footfall close by the pool, or a shadow falling across the water. Providing that they are fed in the same part of the pool regularly they will get to know the routine and almost invariably appear.

It is important to realise that fish are not gross feeders and prefer small amounts of food regularly. During spring and summer they can be fed daily, but no more food should be given than they can comfortably clear up in twenty minutes. Uneaten food falls to the bottom of the pool, starts to decompose and pollute the water, or else develops harmful fungal growth. Almost any balanced fish food is suitable and these are available in three basic types. There is traditional goldfish food which looks like crushed-up biscuit meal and is often multicoloured, flaked food which has the appearance of breakfast cereal, and pelleted foods which look very similar to the compounded pellet food produced for feeding domestic rabbits. Crumb type foods are usually the cheapest, but are not balanced and of doubtful nutritional value. Flaked foods on the other hand usually display an analysis on the container, but have the disadvantage of being light and easily carried away to the far corner of the pool in a breeze. Pelleted foods have an ability to float for a long period of time, but are so large that small fish struggle to devour them, more often than not pushing the pellets round the pool like polo players.

Variety foods like dried flies, dried daphnia and ants

eggs can give diversity in a mundane diet, and these are useful for building up the fish towards the end of the summer and preparing them for winter. The quality of these foods varies considerably and often the ants eggs will be seen to be merely the empty shells of what was a potentially nutritious food. Freeze-dried foods are likely to be more consistent, and while they are a great deal more expensive, the fish fancier usually gets value for money and his fish thrive accordingly.

Routine maintenance

Summer is a good time to propagate many aquatic plants. It is often possible to remove excessive growth and separate this as an individual plant to establish it independently. Algae are often a problem as well and the various means of dealing with this problem are discussed later. Little management is necessary in a well ordered pool. Spring and summer is the time to enjoy this lovely feature.

DO	DO NOT
– Plant aquatic plants and introduce new fish to the pool. – Apply fertiliser as necessary to waterlilies and other aquatic plants. – Feed fish sparingly. – Propagate aquatic plants as necessary.	– Allow an excess of fertiliser to enter the water. – Provide more food than the fish can comfortably clear up in twenty minutes.

A dazzling early summer display of primulas, irises and hostas.

21. The Pool in Autumn and Winter

In the autumn, when the waterlilies fade and the poolside plants turn yellow and limp, thoughts should turn towards preparing the pool for winter. Untidy foliage at the water's edge provides cover for overwintering pests such as waterlily beetle and should be removed as soon as the first frosts turn it brown. Care should be taken when trimming rushes with hollow stems though, as these will drown if cut beneath the water. So it is imperative with this kind of plant that a short length of stem is left showing above the maximum winter water level.

Waterlilies

Waterlilies can be allowed to die back naturally, but any yellow leaves with soft crumbling edges or spreading black blotches should be regarded with suspicion and removed as they may be affected by waterlily leaf spot. Many gardeners feel concern for their waterlilies during the winter, but they need not fear, for as long as there is 9 ins–12 ins (23 cm–30 cm) of water over the crowns they will be perfectly safe. Miniature varieties that may be growing in a shallow rock pool or sink can have the water drained off and the crowns covered with a generous layer of straw for winter protection. A Dutch light or similar covering should be provided as well to prevent the pool or sink refilling with winter rain or snow. Once the fear of sharp frost has passed they can be easily restarted into growth by refilling the pool with water.

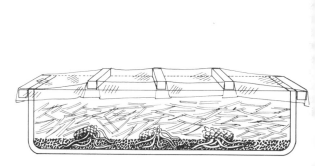

Miniature waterlilies in a sink, covered with straw and a waterproof top.

Free-floating aquatic plants

The majority of free-floating aquatic plants disappear during the winter months, forming turions or winter buds which fall to the bottom of the pool where they remain until the warm spring sunshine stirs them into growth once again. If a few of these are collected before they sink and are placed in a jar of water in a cool airy place, they will start into growth much sooner and can help to combat the troublesome algal growth of early spring by providing much-needed surface shade.

DO	DO NOT
– Clear untidy foliage from poolside plants after frost has turned them brown.	– Cut hollow stemmed subjects below water level.
– Drain sink and tub gardens, protecting the plants with straw and covering the top with a Dutch light.	– Feed fish during winter.
– Collect winter turions of floating plants and keep in jars of water in a cool frost-free place.	– Bang the ice with a heavy instrument to make a hole as this may concuss or kill the fish.
– Feed pool fish with high protein food before severe weather sets in.	
– Float a ball or piece of wood on the surface of the water to absorb pressure from ice and prevent damage to the pool.	
– Ensure that a hole is retained in the ice by use of a pool heater or a pan of hot water which is allowed to melt through.	

Preparing the fish for winter and coping with ice

Ornamental fish must be prepared for winter by judiciously feeding with ants eggs, dried flies, freeze-dried tubifex worms and other high protein foods until the weather turns cold and they cease to be active. No further nourishment need be provided until they are seen swimming about once again during the spring. All popular varieties of pond fish can survive for several months during the winter without feeding, as their body processes slow down in much the same manner as a tree or shrub which becomes dormant. They can also tolerate extreme cold and will not suffer unduly even if temporarily frozen in the ice.

A rubber ball or wood prevents ice damaging the pool

Ice is, of course, the greatest worry a pool owner has during the winter, for it exerts tremendous pressure upon the pool structure and can crack the most expertly laid concrete. The best way of preventing such damage occurring is by floating a piece of wood or child's rubber ball on the water so that the ice exerts pressure against an object capable of expanding and contracting. If a submersible pump is used during the summer, then this can be detached and an electric pool heater installed in its place. This consists of a heated brass rod with a polystyrene float and is perfectly safe to use, keeping an area of water clear of ice in the severest weather.

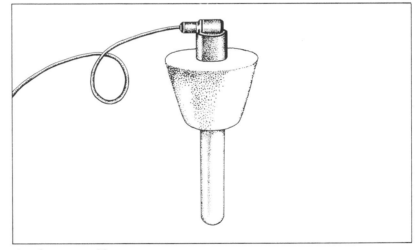

An electric pool heater

Alternatively, during a prolonged harsh spell, when one fears for the safety of the fish, a hole can be made in the ice by placing a pan of boiling water on the surface and allowing it to melt through. This will release any obnoxious gases that have accumulated from the continual decomposition of organic matter on the pool floor and ensure that the fish are not subjected to the shattering shock waves which accompany a well meaning person trying to break the ice with a pick-axe or similar heavy instrument.

Making a hole with a pan of boiling water

22. Scavengers and Snails

There are a number of misconceptions about the role played by scavenging fish and snails in a pool. They will not, as many gardeners suppose, devour mud and stones or completely clear a pool of green slime and algae. What they actually do is to clear up uneaten goldfish food and similar debris, the snails feeding upon various troublesome algae.

Scavenging fish

CATFISH   Many pool owners mistakenly introduce a catfish into their pool in the hope that it will act as a scavenger. While many tropical kinds fulfil this role in an aquarium, the species usually sold for the outdoor pool is both carnivorous and pugnacious, attacking snails, fry and the tails of fancy goldfish. Once in a pool it is almost impossible to catch without draining all the water away. So any of the species offered by aquatics dealers as coldwater catfish should be avoided. These can only be recommended for a solitary life in a coldwater aquarium.

TENCH   The green tench is the most popular fish to be offered as a scavenger. Naturally a floor-dwelling species, it lurks in the depths of the pool feeding on aquatic insect life, plankton, uneaten goldfish food and other undesirable organic matter. It is a handsome fish with a narrow tapering head and short broad olive-green body, although there is a golden form which is often sold for coldwater aquaria. The pool owner intent upon breeding tench can readily distinguish the sexes once the fish are 6 ins (15 cm) or more long. The males have a large ventral fin which reaches to the anal orifice, whereas in the female it is short and weak.

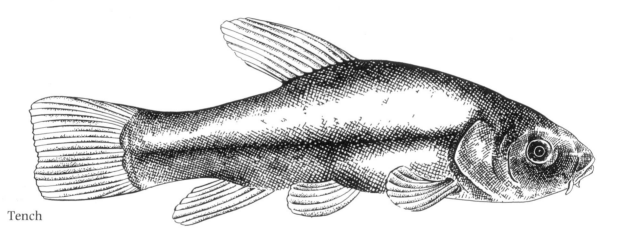

Tench

Freshwater snails

There are literally dozens of different aquatic snails which are suitable for pools and coldwater aquaria, but it is only the ramshorn snail or planorbis which can be readily obtained commercially and will restrain itself from eating plants as well as algae.

RAMSHORN SNAIL   This can be considered as the only snail worth contemplating for the outdoor pool. It is a very distinctive species with a flattened shell like a catherine wheel which it carries in an upright position on its back. The usual kind has a dark shell and a black body, but there are red and white bodied varieties available too. In a pool where all three are present it is the black form that will dominate once breeding commences and eventually the other colours will disappear. Eggs of the ramshorn snail are laid in flat pads of jelly which adhere to the undersides of leaves of aquatic plants. Although there may seem

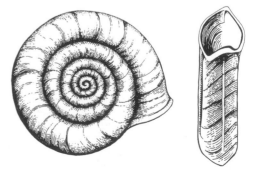

Ramshorn Snail × 2

to be thousands of potential youngsters, these rarely reach maturity as goldfish find the snail eggs a great delicacy.

GREAT POND SNAIL   Although often offered for the garden pool, this snail is best avoided, for it will rarely confine its attentions to algae, preferring to graze on waterlily foliage and the leaves of other succulent aquatics. Apart from this it is an intermediary host between seagulls and fish of a disease that can devastate the fish population. Once in a pool it is difficult to eradicate, the only method being to float fresh lettuce leaves or an old cabbage stalk on the water overnight. Large numbers of pond snails will gather on this vegetation and can be removed and destroyed.

The great pond snail, or freshwater whelk as it is sometimes called, has a tall, spiralled, pointed, greyish or black shell an inch or more high and a greyish-cream body. It lays eggs in large numbers, but in cylinders of jelly rather than flat pads. Often it is these small cigar-shaped cylinders of jelly which lead to trouble in the pool, for they are attached to newly purchased plants and believed by most gardeners to be fish spawn and therefore worth preserving. Careful checking of all newly introduced plants will do much to reduce the population. So too will filling the margins of the pool with plants to prevent birds from bathing in the shallows. Snail eggs are very sticky and can simply be transferred from pool to pool on the feet of local birds.

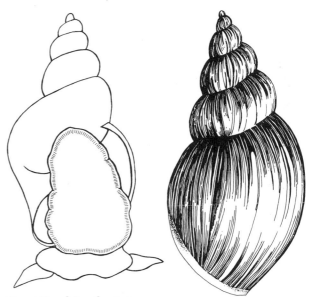

Great Pond Snail × 1.5

Freshwater mussels

These are valuable inhabitants of the well-established pool, sucking in algae-laden water, retaining the algae and discharging clear water. In effect they are living filters. However, they depend upon a good layer of debris or mud on the pool floor through which to crawl, or else they expire. The introduction of a mussel to a newly established pool is folly.

PAINTERS' MUSSEL A fairly small species with a yellowish-green shell conspicuously ringed with brown. Although not as effective as the swan mussel, its life cycle and co-operation with the tiny coldwater fish called the bitterling is legendary, the painters' mussel acting as a foster mother to the young bitterling fry until they are able to swim freely in the pool without protection.

SWAN MUSSEL   This is the commonest species, a dull brownish-green shelled kind, roughly oval in shape, with a white fleshy body. Purchased specimens are rarely more then 2 ins (5 cm) long, but older examples may eventually attain a length of 5 ins (13 cm) in a relatively short space of time.

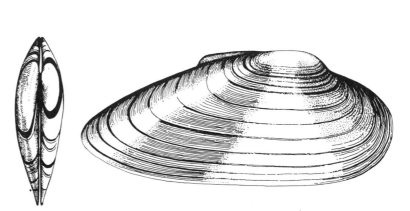

Painters' Mussel (actual size)

23. Pests and Diseases of Aquatic Plants

Although the pests and diseases specific to water plants are few in comparison with most of their land-living cousins, the pool owner is faced with additional difficulties when it comes to their control. The presence of fish creates all manner of problems, for most chemicals are toxic to them, yet the absence of fish leads to the proliferation of undesirable insect life such as gnat and mosquito larvae.

A number of aquatic plants are also susceptible to spray damage, much in the same way as many ferns and greenhouse plants, like cucumbers. Others have such water-repellent foliage that spraying is ineffective, or else the sheer volume of water around the plant dilutes the chemical and renders it useless.

The waterlily aphid

The most troublesome pool pest is the waterlily aphid. In warm humid weather it breeds at a prodigious rate, smothering waterlilies and other succulent aquatics and causing widespread disfigurement of both flower and foliage. Eggs from the late summer brood are laid on the boughs of plum and cherry trees during early autumn and remain there throughout the winter. These hatch the following spring and return to the pool. Here they reproduce rapidly and devour the foliage of aquatic plants. In the autumn a winged generation is once more produced which flies back to the fruit trees to deposit their eggs. The only remedy once they have become established in a pool is to dislodge them from the plants with a strong jet of water and hope that the fish will clear them up. If the pool is freshly established, with no fish present, a contact wash like pyrethrum can be used. Some measure of control can be achieved by spraying all nearby plum and cherry trees with a tar oil wash during the winter months to eliminate the over-wintering population, taking care to drench fissures in the bark where eggs are likely to be laid.

The waterlily beetle

This pest should be attacked during the winter months as well, its hiding places in poolside veg-etation being removed and burned. Although thank-fully of only local occurrence, the waterlily beetle is an important pest that cannot be ignored. The small dark brown beetles and shiny black larvae are found on waterlily foliage, where the latter strip tissue from both flower and foliage, leaving the tattered slimy remains to decay. The adult beetle hibernates during the winter in waterside vegetation and migrates to waterlilies during early June. Here it deposits its eggs in clusters on the leaf surfaces. After a week or so the black larvae with distinctive yellow bellies emerge. These feed on foliage until pupation occurs, either on the waterlily foliage or surrounding aquatic plants.

Apart from the damage caused by their larvae, the adult beetles themselves will be in evidence on the waterlily foliage well in advance of attacks. When noticed, they should be washed from the leaves with a strong jet of clear water so that the fish can clear them up. In the absence of fish, regular spraying with malathion will keep both adults and larvae under control.

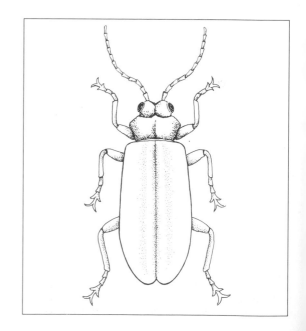

Brown china mark moth

The larva of this moth is more difficult to contain, for not only does it cut and shred the foliage of aquatic plants, but also makes a shelter for itself prior to pupation by sticking down two pieces of leaf which it weaves into a greyish silky cocoon. The eggs are laid during late summer in neat rows along the undersides of floating leaves and hatch after a couple of weeks. The tiny caterpillars burrow into the undersides of the succulent foliage and later make small oval cases out of these leaves. They continue to feed and grow until winter, when most of their food supply is exhausted, becoming dormant and reappearing the following spring to continue the damage until eventually pupating. Minor infestations can be hand picked, but pieces of floating leaf must also be removed as these may well have cocoons attached. When damage is widespread it is easier to completely defoliate the plants and give them a fresh start.

    A close relative, the beautiful china mark moth, is equally destructive, the caterpillars burrowing into the stems of the plants in the formative stage.

Caddis flies

These have similar habits, many species being totally aquatic in their larval stage and swimming around with little shelters made of plant material and other organic debris surrounding them. The flies visit the pool in the cool of the evening, depositing eggs in a mass of jelly which swells up immediately it touches the water. Often this is hooked around submerged foliage in a long cylindrical string or attached to taller plants and allowed to trail in the water. After a couple of weeks the larvae emerge and start to spin their silken cases, at the same time gathering material with which to construct their shelters. While in this state they feed on water plants, devouring all parts equally, until they pupate in the lower pool, to emerge eventually as dull grey or brownish moth-like insects. Control with chemicals is impossible owing to the protective structures which they create around themselves. A healthy population of fish in the pool is the best insurance against a troublesome infestation.

Leaf spots

There are two kinds of waterlily leaf spot commonly encountered. The most widespread appears as dark patches on the foliage which rot through and cause the eventual disintegration of the leaves. It is particularly prevalent during a wet growing season and, as soon as noticed, affected leaves should be removed and burned.

    The other kind, although not so common, is equally destructive. The foliage becomes brown and dry at the edges, eventually crumbling and wasting away. Removal and destruction of all diseased leaves is the only effective cure, although a weak solution of Bordeaux mixture sprayed over the foliage will check its spread.

Root rot

A root rot related to potato blight manifests itself on waterlilies, especially those with dark mottled foliage. The leaf and flower stems become soft and blackened and the root turns evil-smelling and gelatinous. Affected plants should be removed immediately and destroyed.

24. Pests and Diseases of Fish

As one might expect, ornamental fish like any other living creatures are subject to pests and diseases. In the fairly hospitable medium of the garden pool they are perhaps more vulnerable than usual, so a high standard of hygiene is necessary if trouble is to be avoided. Never be tempted to introduce fish or aquatic plants from wild sources as these may carry pests and diseases that will spread like wildfire through a garden pool.

The anchor worm

Although looking rather like a small white worm, this parasite is in fact a crustacean. There are a number of species which attack coldwater fish, but one is specific to goldfish and other members of the carp family. It is a slender, tube-like creature, scarcely $\frac{3}{8}$ inch (1 cm) long with a horrible barbed head which it embeds in the flesh of its host. This gives rise to tumour-like growths, each with a worm protruding, which are often covered in fine algal growth. Anchor worms cannot be withdrawn by pulling, but if an attacked fish is held in a damp cloth and the worms are dabbed with a little paraffin they are quickly killed and can then be removed with tweezers. This causes minimal damage to the fish. It is useful after treatment to dip the fish in a solution of malachite green, as recommended for fungus disease, as this will help prevent secondary infection.

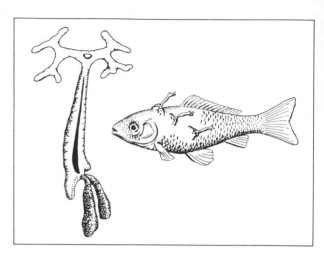

The fish louse

Like the anchor worm, the fish louse is a parasitic crustacean which attaches itself to the bodies of fish causing severe damage. They appear to favour sensitive areas such as the gills and fins where they obviously cause the fish the greatest discomfort. Numerous species are known to fish-keepers, but all look very similar, having a flattened shell-like carapace and feeler-like attachments which they use to cling to their host. Infested fish should be held in a damp cloth and the parasites dabbed with paraffin on a child's paint brush. As the tissue will have been damaged, it is advisable to dip the treated fish in a solution of malachite green to prevent secondary fungal infection.

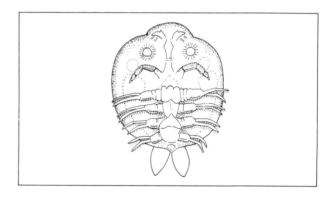

The fish leech

There are a number of leeches common to garden ponds, but only one is a serious pest. This is the fish leech, a rather insignificant creature which has a body consisting of numerous blind sacs, which it fills with blood sucked from its victims. One gorging can last for several months and during this time it just rests amongst aquatic vegetation. It is during the period of feeding that it can cause extensive damage, clinging to its victim until gorged with blood. The attachment of a leech usually renders the fish less active and within a short space of time other leeches become attached. Salt dabbed on a leech attached to a fish will cause it to writhe free. Pulling leeches from fish causes considerable damage. Treated fish should be immersed in a solution of malachite green.

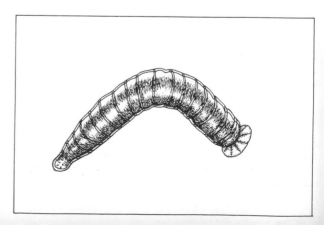

Dropsy

This is a bacterial disease which causes the fish to become distended and the scales to protrude. Indeed, some fish-keepers refer to the disease as scale protrusion. There is no successful cure and the infected fish should be destroyed.

Fin rot and tail rot

A common and very unpleasant disease of which little is known scientifically, except that it is associated with several kinds of bacteria. Infection generally appears on the dorsal fin first of all and, if left unattended, will spread to the other fins and tail reducing them to mere stumps. A white line along the edge of the fin is the first sign of trouble. If at this stage the affected fish can be placed in a solution of one part malachite green to nine parts water for no more than a minute the disease should be arrested. If a fish has gone unnoticed for some time and the disease has spread down the rays of the fin so that they appear frayed, the only option left is to trim the fin to clean tissue with a pair of scissors and then dip the fish in a malachite green solution. When the infection has spread from the fins to the body of the fish it is beyond treatment and the fish should be destroyed.

Fungus

It is seldom that a healthy fish contracts fungus, although after a particularly hard winter in the outdoor pool some of the larger fish will show signs of a slight infection. Usually, though, fungal infection is secondary to some other pest or disease and attacks the open wounds left by that predator or damage sustained in the rough and tumble of the pool. It appears as a cotton wool-like growth which, if left unchecked, will eventually smother the entire fish, invading both the gills and mouth as well. Early treatment almost always produces a cure. Many proprietary fungus cures are on the market, based upon either malachite green or methylene blue, and all are successful when used as a dip for infected fish. Traditionally sea salt used in solution has been the only cure, but this is now outdated as well as being laborious and not reliably successful.

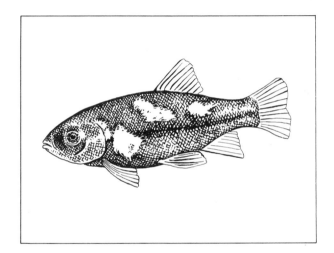

Gill flukes

When a fish is infected with gill flukes it swims in a crazy manner rushing from one side of the pool to the other and banging itself against the planting baskets and pool sides. The fish is obviously greatly disturbed, and while various cures based upon formalin have been suggested they are only partially successful. An affected fish needs putting out of its misery as quickly as possible.

White spot disease

A common and pernicious disease caused by a parasitic protozoa. It is known by scientists as *Ichthyopthirius* and for that reason has been dubbed 'Ich' by aquarists and pond-keepers. A tiny creature, it causes extensive damage to fish by becoming embedded in the skin for at least part of its life cycle. Dozens of parasites will attack a single fish, which then looks as if it has severe white measles. After a while infested fish take on a pinched, starved appearance and eventually die. Severe attacks are rarely curable and badly infested fish should be destroyed. However, mild attacks can be cured by isolating infested fish in a solution of a proprietary white spot cure based upon either acriflavine or quinine salts. White spot is unfortunately a widespread disease, so take great care in the selection of new fish for the pool; these are often the source of infection.

Loss of balance

Sometimes a fish will lose its balance and swim upside down or with its nose pointing downwards. This is a disorder associated with a derangement of the swim bladder or balancing mechanism. Keeping the fish isolated in a stable temperature sometimes solves the problem, enabling the fish to be reintroduced to the pool. Severe cases cannot be treated.

25. Common Pool Problems

Heron

Apart from the various pests and diseases that manifest themselves in fish and plants, there are a number of other problems that regularly arise and which need dealing with carefully.

Discoloured water

By discoloured water we mean water that is other than clear or green. Green water is caused by myriad free-floating algae and will be discussed presently. Discoloured water is that which is brown, black or deep navy-blue and in many cases has a foul smell. Brown water is the result of fish stirring up the compost in plant containers in their quest for food. When a pool is planted as suggested previously, with each container having a generous covering of pea gravel, this problem rarely arises. Sometimes if the soil used to fill the containers is rather light it drifts out through the lattice-work sides of the container. This can be prevented by lining the container initially with a square of hessian to retain soil but allow water to percolate and roots to break out. If plants have been planted in containers without a generous top dressing of gravel, then regretfully the pool must be cleaned out and re-planting undertaken.

Water that is blue-black, black or has a thick whitish scum or oily film around the edges is usually polluted by a decaying inhabitant or a build-up of decomposing leaves from nearby trees. It usually has a foul smell, is very low in oxygen and regular deaths of fish and snails will be occurring. A thorough clean-out is the only recommendation that can be made and this will usually lead to the discovery of the offending pollutant. The sides of the pool should be thoroughly scrubbed and it is advantageous if the pool can then be left to dry out in the open air for a day or two. Any plants that look in good health can be returned in good clean soil in containers that have received a vigorous scrubbing.

Coping with algae

Aquatic algae are probably the greatest bane of the pool keeper's life. They occur in a wide range of forms from the free-floating, dust-like kinds to the clinging mermaid's hair and the long filamentous spirogyra. The minutest forms are suspended in the water and if a hand is passed through, a greenish smear remains. Filamentous kinds are more substantial and can be pulled out of the water by the handful, while the mermaid's hair clings to baskets and the poolside and can be removed in tufts if pulled sharply.

Control of the free-floating kinds is not difficult with an algaecide based upon potassium permanganate, but its effect is short-lived and, if not carefully used during warm weather, will turn the water yellow. Filamentous algae can be controlled with algaecides based upon copper sulphate, but it is important that all dead algae are removed after treatment to prevent de-oxygenation of the water. On no account should straight chemicals be used by the uninitiated.

The algal controls described are not permanent and do not replace the natural balance which produces sweet mellow water and healthy conditions. They are essentially temporary aids for a new pool until the submerged plants have become established and can compete on an equal footing. They can also be used in difficult periods in an established pool, particularly at the time in spring when an algal bloom develops before the higher plants have really got growing. Clear water at this time is not only pleasing to observe, but permits the submerged plants to make more rapid growth.

Dealing with a heron

Even pool owners who live in suburbia will be visited from time to time by a heron. It seems that nothing escapes the eagle eye of this majestic, but destructive bird. Very often the disappearance of fish from a garden pool is something of a mystery, for the heron visits early in the morning before most people are about. It fishes by standing in or beside the water, making a stab for its unfortunate victim and usually coming out with its prize. Large goldfish are regularly taken and young fish are equally vulnerable. Some garden centres sell special netting for covering the pool to prevent the attention of herons, but these are unsightly and create all kinds of difficulties when surrounding vegetation grows through. The simplest and most effective method of control is by erecting a series of short canes around the perimeter of the pool about 6 ins (15 cm) high from which black garden cotton or fishing line is fastened to give the effect of a low fence. When the heron goes fishing he naturally walks towards the water, but his legs come in contact with the line which he cannot see. After making several attempts to reach the pool and meeting the same hazard each time, he generally goes in search of pastures – or pools – new.

Index

Philip Swindells, F.L.S., is superintendent of Harlow Car, the gardens of the Northern Horticultural Society. He broadcasts regularly on radio and television, and is the author of *Ferns for Garden and Greenhouse, Making the Most of Water Gardening, Waterlilies*, and *The Water Gardener's Handbook*.